T0351616

365 DAYS of Friendship

DEVOTIONS ON HOW TO BE A GOOD FRIEND

BroadStreet
PUBLISHING

BroadStreet Publishing Group, LLC.
Savage, Minnesota, USA
Broadstreetpublishing.com

365 DAYS OF FRIENDSHIP

© 2022 by BroadStreet Publishing®

978-1-4245-6543-6
978-1-4245-6544-3 ebook

Devotional entries composed by Sara Perry.

Design and typesetting by Garborg Design Works | garborgdesign.com
Editorial services by Michelle Winger | literallyprecise.com

Printed in China.

22 23 24 25 26 27 28 7 6 5 4 3 2 1

Sweet friendships refresh the soul and awaken our hearts with joy.

Proverbs 27:9 tpt

INTRO

One of the most precious things about life is the gift of friendship. Receiving a kind word from a friend can make all the difference in your day. Good friends believe the best about you and often have an inspired, beautifully timed way of expressing it. The sincere words of an encouraging friend bring life.

As you read these devotions and Scriptures, be inspired to live with gratitude in your heart and praise on your lips. Meditate on friendships that produce life and peace. Evaluate each day in the light of God's truth and thank him for your good friends. As you quiet yourself before him, be filled with his life-giving joy so you can pour it out on others.

Speak life into a friend each day of the year and brighten the world with love.

JANUARY

Perfume and incense
bring joy to the heart,
and the pleasantness
of a friend
springs from their
heartfelt advice.

PROVERBS 27:9 NIV

UNCONDITIONAL LOVE

A dear friend will love you no matter what,
and a family sticks together through all kinds of trouble.

PROVERBS 17:17 TPT

Friends are among the greatest gifts we receive in this life. A trusted friend who we can turn to, no matter how well or how poorly we are doing, is a treasure. A friend who will receive us, support us, and lift us up is a gift greater than anything we could create with our hands.

Who are the friends in your life that show up when it matters? The ones who won't judge you or push you away when you are struggling to keep up with life? Who are the friends that you show up for? Take time to give thanks to God for each one, for they are glimmers of his pursuing heart in flesh and bones.

A FRIEND IN DEED

*Send a text of gratitude and love to a dear friend,
letting them know how much you appreciate them.*

COMPASSIONATE COMFORT

Praise be to the God and Father of our Lord Jesus Christ, the Father of compassion and the God of all comfort.

2 Corinthians 1:3 niv

When we are in pain, going through trials and struggles, God does not demand that we suck it up or look on the bright side. He does not bypass our hard emotions. He meets us right in the midst of them with compassion and comfort.

Can the same be said of us in our relationships? Do we dare leave space for discomfort in ourselves as we allow another to experience the depth of their sorrows without the need to fix it or move on quickly? May we be people of compassion and comfort, offering safety, support, and peace to our friends in their sorrow. May we listen with open hearts and show up in tangible ways that offer relief and support.

A FRIEND IN DEED

Take time to listen to a friend without changing the subject.

CHOOSE KINDNESS

He who withholds kindness from a friend
forsakes the fear of the Almighty.

JOB 6:14 ESV

Kindness is one of the fruits of God's Spirit. It is more than being superficially nice to others; it is a heart posture of generosity and a consideration moved into action. Choosing to intentionally and voluntarily move in kind and friendly gestures starts with our hearts and our minds. As we live out our intentions, our character is revealed.

Clear communication is a way to show kindness. We cannot expect others to read our minds and know what we need from them. When we withhold our honesty, our hearts may grow bitter. This makes it harder on us and on those around us. May we have the discernment to know what needs to be said in love and what can be let go of. May we choose clarity and connection over passive acts that promote disconnection.

A FRIEND IN DEED

Have an honest conversation that you've been avoiding.

HEART OF GRATITUDE

We ought always to thank God for you, brothers and sisters, and rightly so, because your faith is growing more and more, and the love all of you have for one another is increasing.

2 THESSALONIANS 1:3 NIV

When we witness growth and maturity in those we love, we celebrate with them! When we watch our loved ones grow in understanding and choose to move in mercy, our hearts may grow with gratitude. May we look through the lens of love today, recognizing where the steady faith of others has bolstered our own.

Let's pray and give thanks to God for faithful friends. Let's honor the love that others show, not only to us, but in service to others. Let's be loud supporters of our friends, cheering them on in love and encourage them to keep doing the good that they are doing. Let's increase our own love and service as we celebrate them.

A FRIEND IN DEED

Congratulate and celebrate a friend!

PRAYERS OF THANKS

You know that I've been called to serve the God of my fathers with a clean conscience. Night and day I pray for you, thanking God for your life!

2 TIMOTHY 1:3 TPT

There are people in our lives that are like beacons of hope whenever we think of them. Who are the people that cultivate gratitude in your heart? Which friends make you overflow with thanksgiving? Perhaps there are friends who have been steady supports in the tumultuous times of your life. Perhaps it is a friend who brings you laughter and joy when you need it most. Maybe there are friends that just get you, and you them, and that is enough.

Take some time to pray for these friends today, praying for their strength, encouragement, and breakthrough. Let gratitude lead you to the throne of your Father, and partner with his heart as you pray over your friends.

A FRIEND IN DEED

*Call a close friend and thank them
for how they've enriched your life.*

CHOOSE CAREFULLY

Godly people are careful about the friends they choose.
But the way of sinners leads them down the wrong path.

PROVERBS 12:26 NIRV

Our character is built in the company of those we surround ourselves with. Who are our closest friends? Who do we spend the most time with? How does their influence show up in our lives? We cannot escape the impact of others' ideas, choices, attitudes, and lifestyles on our own mindsets.

May we be intentional with those we open up to and trust with the vulnerable parts of ourselves. Let's choose close friends who are loving, reliable, and kind, who can speak honestly with us. May we cultivate integrity in our own lives, refusing to gossip or slander others. We can be trustworthy and true, seeking to become our best selves and encouraging others to do the same.

A FRIEND IN DEED

*Connect with a trusted friend today
and tell them what's been going on with you.*

EVERY TIME

Every time I think of you,
I give thanks to my God.

PHILIPPIANS 1:3 NLT

We all know that person, the one who, whenever we think of them, gives us a feeling of gratitude and joy. It is a gift to know them and to be known by them. It is so easy to become distracted by the disappointments in life and in relationships. Instead of being overwhelmed by reasons to give up hope in humanity, let's turn our attention to the gifts of grace that meet us in our friends.

Instead of focusing on the discouraging failures of others, let's home in on the gracious attributes of those we love. Who do we give thanks for? What is it about them that fills us with joy? Let's look for ways to express our gratitude and be people who bring joy and peace to others.

A FRIEND IN DEED

Pray a blessing over those who bring joy to your heart and life.

REASON TO REJOICE

"When he arrives, he will call together his friends and neighbors, saying, 'Rejoice with me because I have found my lost sheep.'"

LUKE 15:6 NLT

There are seasons in friendships that echo the seasons of nature. We may not see eye-to-eye the way we used to, or they may be going through a wintering of the soul where they do not have the capacity to show up in the same ways they once could. There are so many reasons why we may not feel as close to beloved friends as we once did.

Can we follow the example of Jesus and fight for the relationships that matter? Let's keep pursuing those we love in times when they are struggling even when they feel far from us. When we think of our own dark nights, the ones who stick with us through thick and thin are the trusted friends we can rely on. May we give grace and receive it with joy, knowing that true friends are worth fighting for.

A FRIEND IN DEED

Reach out to a friend you've lost touch with.

GREAT PROMISES

He has granted to us his precious and very great promises,
so that through them you may become partakers of the
divine nature, having escaped from the corruption that is in
the world because of sinful desire.

2 PETER 1:4 ESV

The most fulfilling gifts and promises are found within the
context of relationship. What good is our own perceived
success if we are alone in it? The love of Christ always
reaches out. It is expansive rather than confining. In the
same way, what is love without a recipient? We receive the
love of Christ, and we offer it to others.

May we be people of our word, who keep our promises. It
is important to keep the promises we make to ourselves
as well as those we make to others. May we be people of
integrity, living in honesty without the need for perfection.
May we live, move, and breathe the love of God in all that
we do!

A FRIEND IN DEED

Follow through on what you said you would do for a friend.

CELEBRATING WITH OTHERS

I thank God because in Christ you have been made rich in every way, in all your speaking and in all your knowledge.

1 CORINTHIANS 1:5 NCV

When our friends succeed, do we celebrate with them, or do we compare ourselves to them? May we be champions of one another, rejoicing in each other's triumphs as well as sharing each other's burdens. We may easily relate to our friends in the disappointments but find it more difficult to celebrate their successes.

The success of a friend does not mean there is less room for our own. May we be intentional about rejoicing with them, remembering that as we lift each other up, our time of celebration will also come. There is no need to compare our wins with each other! True friendship is as present in the joy as it is in the heartache.

A FRIEND IN DEED

*Make a point of celebrating
a friend's achievement or triumph!*

STAYING IN THE LIGHT

This is the message we have heard from him and declare
to you: God is light; in him there is no darkness at all.

1 JOHN 1:5 NIV

God is not divisive, he is not moody, and he is not petty. We
are only human, and we will exhibit these traits from time
to time, but let's not lurk in the shadows of judgment and
hypercriticism, looking for ways to tear others down. When
we stay in the light, as God is in the light, we are able to
look past our emotions to the roots of them; from that place
we can extend compassion both to ourselves and to others.

When we fellowship with God, spending time in his
presence, we experience the light of his love, peace,
compassion, kindness, and mercy in our souls. There is joy
in his presence and there is freedom in his affection. May
we choose to remain in him, leaving behind the habits that
drag us into shame, fear, and self-protection.

A FRIEND IN DEED

*Ask the Lord what habits keep you
from loving others well.*

PART OF GOD'S FAMILY

God decided in advance to adopt us into his own family
by bringing us to himself through Jesus Christ.
This is what he wanted to do, and it gave him great pleasure.

EPHESIANS 1:5 NLT

We cannot choose the family that we're born into, but there
are friends that become as close to us as our own flesh and
blood. This is the family we choose. What a gift it is to find
sisters and brothers who are as dear to us as any we are
related to. No one is excluded from this kind of connection!

The family of God is not perfect, just as any human family
is flawed. But it is a place where love and forgiveness,
compassion and restoration, are exemplified. Just as we are
not close to everyone in our earthly families, we do not
have to be bosom buddies with every believer. May we give
ourselves and others the grace to choose close friends and
trustworthy confidants.

A FRIEND IN DEED

Tell a trusted friend what their friendship means to you.

FULL OF WISDOM

If any of you is lacking in wisdom, ask God,
who gives to all generously and ungrudgingly,
and it will be given you.

JAMES 1:5 NRSV

Being in relationship with others will always require humility, love, forgiveness, kindness, and patience. The longer we live, the more we will see this is true. When we are lacking wisdom in our friendships, let's turn to the Lord who answers our cries. He has all the wisdom we need to show us how to live. Through Christ's example and teachings, we catch a glimpse of the glory of God's grace.

God's Word is practical. His wisdom teaches us how to live with love as our leader. God is generous and kind, always giving his grace freely to us. Instead of throwing our hands up in exasperation when we don't know what to do, let's look to him. He will lead us and teach us in perfect, loving wisdom. He knows exactly what to do and just what we need!

A FRIEND IN DEED

Pray for wisdom in your friendships.

ALREADY KNOWN

"Before I formed you in the womb I knew you,
before you were born I set you apart."

JEREMIAH 1:5 NIV

Hopefully, you are already acquainted with how completely known and thoroughly loved you are. Even when others misunderstand us, God knows our hearts and intentions. He knows what we could never express to another in words. Gloriously, this is true of each one of us! This means that God knows our friends as intimately as he knows us.

May we look through the lens of God's perspective as we consider our friends today. What we do not understand, God does. What we fail to grasp, God does not miss. May our hearts expand and soften in compassion as we consider how loved we are, and how loved those around us are, by the King of kings and Lord of lords.

A FRIEND IN DEED

*Give a friend the benefit of the doubt
and ask questions to better understand them.*

HE'S STILL WORKING

I am confident of this very thing, that He who began a good work in you will perfect it until the day of Christ Jesus.

PHILIPPIANS 1:6 NASB

In the in-between times in life that feel like a waiting room, let's not lose hope. The beauty of friendship is that even when we feel our own hope dwindling, someone else can hold us up.

Is there a friend you know who is in a time of struggle? Don't force them to be positive about their situation but let them know that you have hope for their breakthrough. Pray for them and encourage them with practical acts of lovingkindness. If God gives you a word of encouragement, share it with them. Let them know that you believe God is still working on their behalf. Be a gift of hope when they cannot conjure up any of their own.

A FRIEND IN DEED

Tell a friend that you are praying for them and encourage them with hope.

UNBROKEN FELLOWSHIP

If we keep living in the pure light that surrounds him,
we share unbroken fellowship with one another, and the
blood of Jesus, his Son, continually cleanses us from all sin.

1 JOHN 1:7 TPT

When we walk in the lifegiving light of fellowship with
the Spirit of God, we are united in his love. Nothing can
separate us from the love of God in Christ. This is what
Paul says in Romans, and it is echoed in John's statement in
this verse. Nothing in this world has the power to diminish
God's love. Nothing can come between us and his love.

In the same way that nothing can separate us from the
love of God, let's not let anything divorce us from our
compassion for others. First John 4:19 says, "our love
for others is our grateful response to the love God first
demonstrated to us." Let us live out our love as a sign of our
gratitude. Jesus is worthy of every sacrificial movement of
mercy we make.

Choose kindness when faced with the choice to judge another.

POWER OF THE SPIRIT

God will never give you the spirit of fear,
but the Holy Spirit who gives you mighty power,
love, and self-control.

2 TIMOTHY 1:7 TPT

Have you ever been afraid to tell a close friend the truth of something going on in your life? Perhaps you have been struggling in a relationship, or you have changed in ways that you assume they won't understand. Instead of letting fear keep you from being open, being vulnerable with a trusted friend can open the gate for deeper understanding.

Let's not let self-protection or fears of rejection and being misunderstood keep us from being open with those who have proven trustworthy in our lives. We cannot control their response, but if they have shown us love and understanding before, chances are they will do it again. Fear causes us to hide and shrink, but love causes us to grow and connect.

A FRIEND IN DEED

If there is something you have been withholding from a trusted friend, take a step in vulnerability today.

HOPEFUL REMINDERS

You, my delightfully loved friends,
remember the prophecies
of the apostles of our Lord Jesus,
the Anointed One.

JUDE 1:17 TPT

Have you ever watched a friend go through a transition where they lost their footing and couldn't remember who they were? These times in life happen to all of us, but the honesty, support, and encouragement of those who know us well can make all the difference.

May we be the type of friends who hold each other up with the truth. May we encourage each other with reminders of who we are and who we are becoming. Let's not let mistakes define us. Let's not let the doubts of our lives muddy our relationships. There is beauty, clarity, and kindness in reminding each other of who we have been created to be. Let's call out each other's gifts and personality traits. And let's give room for growth, change, and expansion.

A FRIEND IN DEED

*Write a note to a friend of all
that you know to be true of them.*

LIFEGIVING WISDOM

The seeds of good deeds become a tree of life;
a wise person wins friends.

PROVERBS 11:30 NLT

Acts of kindness do not just benefit the receiver; they also profit the giver. One who is focused on living a life of integrity is not just concerned with their own life but also with the effects their choices have on others.

May we be honest and true, loving and kind, reflecting the love of Christ in how we live. Let's choose generosity in every area, living large with loving acts. Let's build oaks of righteousness with our actions, following through on our good intentions. May we be full of wisdom that sees beyond the narrow views we have been taught to uphold and let's dig deeper into the connective truth that is all around us. Let's build our lives on the wisdom of God's kingdom, for he knows what he is doing.

A FRIEND IN DEED

Run an errand for a friend.

CHOOSE TRUST

The LORD is good,
a refuge in times of trouble.
He cares for those who trust in him.

NAHUM 1:7 NIV

We are never alone in our times of discouragement. God does not leave us in our great need. He is close with help, and he cares for us. Let's remember how lovingly he attends to us. We can trust him with all that we are, all that we hope for, and all that we cannot control.

May we also be people who let others in during our times of need. May we be trustworthy and true to our friends when they need a helping hand. We can reflect the love of Christ in both the receiving and giving of care. May we not neglect the part we play in the kingdom of Christ's love! Let's find shelter in the kindness of trusted friends as often as we offer it to others.

A FRIEND IN DEED

Ask for help in an area where you are overwhelmed.

INEXPRESSIBLE JOY

Though you have not seen Him, you love Him, and though you do not see Him now, but believe in Him, you greatly rejoice with joy inexpressible and full of glory.

1 PETER 1:8 NASB

Though we have not seen God face-to-face, we know him. We know him through his unchanging merciful nature and through his character displayed in Christ. How could we but love him when he has lavished his love upon us?

In the same way that we have joy in the nature of God, may we recognize the traits of our friends that also bring us gladness. As we spend time with our friends, knowing the curve of their smiles and the lilt of their laughs, we can rejoice in the goodness of their character and how it enriches our lives! May we find that the more we take delight in the Lord, the more we appreciate those around us.

A FRIEND IN DEED

Think about what traits you appreciate in your friends.

LOOKING BEYOND

"I am the Alpha and the Omega," says the LORD God,
"who is, and who was, and who is to come, the Almighty."

REVELATION 1:8 NIV

Our lives on this earth have a beginning and an end. They
are limited, yet through Christ we are promised eternity
in his loving presence and everlasting kingdom. Before we
were born, God knew us. Long after we are gone, he will
know us still.

The memory of a loved one does not diminish with their
passing. They live on in our hearts, through grief and
through hope. May we not take for granted the time
we have with our beloved friends and family. Let's be
intentional about sharing, not only the connection of life
with them, but also the things we love and appreciate about
them. Time is fleeting though love is not. Let us live in the
present moment fully while still looking beyond to what is
to come.

A FRIEND IN DEED

Call a beloved friend and tell them how much you love them.

PROMOTERS OF PEACE

Make no friendship with a man given to anger,
nor go with a wrathful man,
lest you learn his ways
and entangle yourself in a snare.

PROVERBS 22:24-25 ESV

Jesus said in John 14:27, "Peace I leave with you; my peace I give to you…let not your hearts be troubled, nor let them be afraid." If we want to be like Christ, we will live with the promise of his peace lining our hearts and our choices. Let us be people who build our relationships on the foundation of Christ's barrier-breaking love.

No one wants to be around a person who is prone to violent and angry outbursts. That is not a friendship based on the security of connection. That is not to say we can never feel anger or be friends with those who do. The text is speaking of a person who is disposed to acting angrily. May we dwell in the peace of Jesus, seeking restoration and truth even when we are passionate about our opinions.

A FRIEND IN DEED

Be a safe space for a friend, seeking to understand their view without attempting to change their mind.

REMEMBER THE HOPE

He delivered us from such a deadly peril,
and he will deliver us.
On him we have set our hope
that he will deliver us again.

2 CORINTHIANS 1:10 ESV

Jesus, our great deliverer, has not forgotten the promises he has made. He has not fallen asleep to our situations, and he has certainly not grown apathetic toward our need of him. May we remember the hope of his salvation, the promise of his resurrection power, and the breakthrough of his love in our lives. He is not finished working out his goodness in us.

Can you think of a friend struggling with discouragement today? Perhaps you are the one who has been deep in the throes of depression. This is not a failure of faith; it is a part of the journey of life. There is hope today for any who need it. There is encouragement for our souls. There is life, joy, and peace in the presence of God. May we find relief there.

A FRIEND IN DEED

*Encourage a struggling friend with a prayer
or a word of hope today.*

KINGDOM OF LIGHT

He has delivered us from the power of darkness and conveyed us into the kingdom of the Son of His love.

COLOSSIANS 1:13 NKJV

In the kingdom of Christ, we have freedom in the redemption that Jesus has offered us. We are free to walk, live, and move in his lifegiving light. We leave behind the shame and fear of the darkness of this world and are liberated! He sets us in wide open spaces where his love leads us. There is no reason to live with the fear of misstep or the guilt of not being perfect, for Christ is our perfection and we are in him.

Are you wracked by guilt in any of your friendships? Perhaps you feel as if you should be able to give them more time. Maybe you think that too long a period has passed to reach out. Instead of continuing to pull away with assumptions, reach out in love. Don't let another day go by where you allow fear to keep you from connecting with those who are important to you.

A FRIEND IN DEED

Reach out to a friend who has been estranged from you.

JUST LIKE US

The Living Expression became a man and lived among us!
And we gazed upon the splendor of his glory, the glory of
the One and Only who came from the Father overflowing
with tender mercy and truth!

JOHN 1:14 TPT

What a wonderful truth it is that Jesus took on flesh and
humanity to walk the earth with us, like us, and for us.
He revealed the heart of the Father in a way that we most
desperately needed. Keeping the rules of religion may help
with morality, but it does not set us free or save us. Christ
came to show us the way to the liberty of relationship with
the Father, all while experiencing the fullness of the human
experience.

Do we approach our friendships with the same kind of
grace that Jesus offers us, or do we expect perfection? If
we are not willing to communicate clearly with others, we
cannot expect those who are different from us to know
what we expect, feel, need, or want. Let's follow the example
of Christ and let grace line our hearts and relationships.

A FRIEND IN DEED

Be clear in your conversations today.

PRACTICE PATIENCE

Jesus Christ might display his perfect patience as an
example to those who were to believe in him for eternal life.

1 TIMOTHY 1:16 ESV

Learning patience when we're young is tedious and
certainly not the strong suit of many. Our culture does not
promote the goodness found in waiting; many times, we
are offered shortcuts and instant gratification. But this does
nothing for the growth of our character!

Proverbs 19:11 says, "a person's wisdom yields patience; it is to
one's glory to overlook an offense" (NIV). If wisdom produces
patience, then as we mature in faith and in life, we come to
understand that it is to our benefit to learn endurance through
hard and dry seasons. This is as true in friendships as in any
other area. May we be those who learn to overlook offenses
that were never about us in the first place.

A FRIEND IN DEED

Forgive a friend for a slight
and give them the benefit of the doubt.

GRATEFUL HEART

I have not stopped giving thanks for you,
remembering you in my prayers.

EPHESIANS 1:16 NIV

In certain seasons of our lives, we may forget the
importance of continuing to cultivate the friendships that
have meant so much to us. When we go into our own
wintering of sorts, whether that be grief over a loss, a family
crisis, or an illness that takes over our lives, we may find it
hard to focus on little else than our own pain.

It is true that what we give our attention to, we make room
for in our hearts. Wherever we find ourselves today, may
we cultivate a heart of connection to our friends. Even if
the only energy we have is to think of them and give thanks
to God for them, that's a good place to begin. Let's give
gratitude, choosing to recognize who has bettered our lives
for knowing them.

A FRIEND IN DEED

Give thanks to God in prayer for your beloved friends!

RELY ON CHRIST

Christ didn't send me to baptize,
but to preach the Good News—
and not with clever speech,
for fear that the cross of Christ
would lose its power.

1 CORINTHIANS 1:17 NLT

Jesus taught that we should rely on the Father in all things. He instructed that we should not worry about what we will eat or wear, or where we will live. God already knows our needs, and he will provide for us. When we submit our lives to him, we do not only trust him to work through us in spiritual ways but also in practical ways.

You don't need the perfect thing to say to a suffering friend. You do not have to be clever, funny, or in a happy mood in order to connect with someone. Just be yourself, rely on Christ to give you wisdom when you don't know what to do, and show up. Let your heart lead in love and be humble and open. The rest will come!

A FRIEND IN DEED

Choose to show up as you are in your friendships today.

HEARTS OF HOPE

I pray that the eyes of your heart may be enlightened, so that you will know what is the hope of His calling, what are the riches of the glory of His inheritance in the saints.

EPHESIANS 1:18 NASB

When we believe and hope for the best for those around us, we carry our faith into our relationships. There is a greater hope waiting for each of us in the kingdom of Christ. Though we walk through trials and storms of many kinds, they are not indicators of our place in God's kingdom.

Do we pray and encourage our friends with hope when they are losing their own? When they cannot see the way out of the dark, we can stand with them and keep watch. Let's pray for their comfort, their peace, their understanding, and their breakthrough. What are friends for if not to hold each other up when we cannot stand on our own?

A FRIEND IN DEED

Reach out to a friend who is struggling.

IN CHRIST

All of God's promises have been fulfilled in Christ with a resounding "Yes!" And through Christ, our "Amen" ascends to God for his glory.

2 CORINTHIANS 1:20 NLT

God does not go back on his promises. Even when we fail—and others are sure to fail us as well—God does not waver. He is the perfect promise keeper. There is grace upon grace lavished on us; may we offer this kind of grace in our relationships! Let's aim to be people of our word, keeping our promises and admitting when it is impossible to do so.

May we learn to only say yes to what we can actually do, without burning ourselves out or stretching ourselves thin. A "no" given with confidence and kindness is as important as a willing yes. Whether we offer a yes or no today in our friendships, may we do so with intentionality, clarity, and love.

A FRIEND IN DEED

Be clear with your responses today.

FEBRUARY

A friend loves you all the time,
and a brother helps
in time of trouble.

PROVERBS 17:17 NCV

FASTEN YOUR FAITH

It is through him that you now believe in God,
who raised him from the dead and glorified him,
so that you would fasten your faith and hope in God alone.

1 PETER 1:21 TPT

What is your faith rooted in? Where do your deepest hopes lie? Is it in the fulfillment of dreams, reaching goals, and escaping pain? Or is your ultimate hope in the promises of God? If you find yourself at a loss, don't let shame keep you from directing your heart to the Lord today. He knows how feeble you are. He lovingly welcomes you, no matter how you come to him.

Take some time to read through Jesus' life and words in the gospels. He crosses cultural boundaries and tells of the mercy of the Father. He gives hope to weary hearts and offers rest for those who are burdened by the worries of life. Find respite in him today and encourage your friends to do the same.

A FRIEND IN DEED

*Lean into Christ and let that be the place you fill up;
your relationships will benefit from your soul's rest.*

KEPT IN LOVE

Keep yourselves in the love of God,
waiting for the mercy of our Lord Jesus Christ
that leads to eternal life.

JUDE 1:21 ESV

We never grow out of the love of God. There is no point in our life or faith journey where his love becomes irrelevant. It is always overflowing and expanding. Even as we wait for the fullness of Christ's mercy to be revealed in the earth, we get to practice living his mercy out in our lives and relationships.

A couple of verses later in Jude, the author instructs the reader to keep being compassionate to those with doubts and to be merciful over and over again. Though we may run out of our own supply of patience and love, God never does, and he is our source! May we throw every excuse that keeps us from being merciful to others out the window, for the kingdom of God is never ending in rich mercy, and we will be known as his own by our love (John 13:35).

A FRIEND IN DEED

*Choose to extend mercy rather than judgment
to those around you.*

GLORIOUS PROMISE

All glory to God, who is able to keep you from falling away and will bring you with great joy into his glorious presence without a single fault.

JUDE 1:24 NLT

What a glorious hope we have in Christ! He cleanses us from our unrighteousness in the perfection of his own love. Nothing could stop him from pouring it out; even death was not a hindrance to the love of Christ. The power that raised him from the dead broke every chain that held us captive in this world. We are liberated in his mercy, and we are made completely whole and new in him.

What joy awaits us. Wherever there is love, whenever there is restoration, when we support one another and help each other by meeting each other's needs and being an emotional support, we reflect the joy of being part of God's family. Let's not give up leaning into the joyful glimpses of communion that we have here and now!

A FRIEND IN DEED

Help a friend out and let their joy become your own!

HIGHER WISDOM

The foolishness of God is wiser than human wisdom,
and the weakness of God is stronger than human strength.

1 CORINTHIANS 1:25 NIV

The understanding of humanity is, and always will be,
within this life, partial. We cannot see or comprehend
the totality of the realities of the universe. We are not all
inclined in mathematics or music comprehension. May
we live with the humble awareness that we see in part and
only know in part, and when we learn more, may we admit
where our understanding was limited before.

God is full of wisdom, and he never makes a mistake. We
cannot venture to know everything about him. We cannot
claim to have his ineffable knowledge. We must keep the
right perspective in our hearts and attitudes. As we grow
in understanding and as we fellowship with the Lord, he
teaches us. May we remain humble and teachable, not only
with God, but also with others.

A FRIEND IN DEED

Be open to learning something new from a friend.

LAID DOWN LOVE

"No one has greater love than this,
to lay down one's life for one's friends."

JOHN 15:13 NRSV

These are Jesus' words to his disciples. Directly before this instruction, Jesus says, "This is my commandment, that you love one another as I have loved you." If we think that we have no room to grow in our relationships or in how we show love to others, let's take a moment to consider whether our love looks like Jesus' own.

If we do what he commands us to do, Jesus says we will be known as his friends. We partner with his purposes when we commit our lives to loving each other the way he loves us. This is no small ask, and no little task. But he is with us through it all, guiding us and offering us the strength and grace of his Spirit. May we dare to live out our love in sacrificial acts and not just in safely measured methods.

A FRIEND IN DEED

*Sacrificially show love to a friend today.
Let it cost you something.*

THE HIGH ROAD

When we are slandered, we reply as friends;
we have become as the scum of the world,
the dregs of all things, even until now.

1 Corinthians 4:13 nasb

We live in a world that promotes revenge. If someone is mean to us, we should be mean to them. If they slander us, we should defend ourselves and make known that they are in the wrong. This is not to say that there is no place for accountability, justice, or truth. Of course there is!

Often when someone attacks us, it doesn't have much to do with us at all; rather, it's based on the attacker's own fears, biases, or trauma. May we learn to first give grace when others would bristle or fight. Let's follow the loving lead of Christ and let our responses be gentle, all while reminding ourselves that our worth is in the Lord and not in another's opinion of us.

A FRIEND IN DEED

Choose to take the high road in your interactions today.

UNTO GOD

We speak as messengers approved by God to be entrusted
with the Good News. Our purpose is to please God, not
people. He alone examines the motives of our hearts.

1 Thessalonians 2:4 nlt

What a relief it is to know that God examines the motives
of our hearts. Though perhaps to some it does not feel like a
relief. The truth is that God knows when we are trying our
best, just as surely as he knows when we are reacting out of
our pain. Either way, we can trust him in his mercy to hold us.

We cannot please everyone. That is as true of those in our
lives as it is in greater society. We each have our own ideas
of what we should do in various circumstances. We each
have personal preferences, and these do not align with
everyone else's. Instead of trying to please everyone, work
to live with integrity, being true to who God has created
you to be.

A FRIEND IN DEED

Look to God for your acceptance today.

UNDER LOVE'S BANNER

He has brought me to his banquet hall,
And his banner over me is love.

SONG OF SOLOMON 2:4 NASB

Sharing a meal can be one of the most mundane and yet familial acts we do with those who are close to us. The Word of God illustrates intimacy through a feast in this passage. We have a place at the banqueting table of our God.

Who has a place at our table? Who do we share our homes and meals with? No matter what we serve, whether we make it from scratch or pick it up ready-made, may love's banner be over our hearts and homes. Let's lean into the vulnerability of sharing ourselves with our friends. Some of the best conversations happen over a dinner table. Let's break bread with our close friends just as Jesus did with his disciples. Let's feast together and let the nourishing of our bodies lead to enrichment of our hearts and souls.

A FRIEND IN DEED

Invite a friend over for a meal.

LIVED OUT LOVE

> If anyone obeys his word, love for God is truly made
> complete in them. This is how we know we are in him.
>
> 1 JOHN 2:5 NIV

Our love doesn't mean much of anything if it isn't apparent in our choices, lifestyles, and interactions. It would be like someone saying, "I prefer to dye my hair red," but they always have blonde hair. What difference does it make if that's the preference, but they don't follow through on it? This is a silly example, but you get the point.

If we claim to live in the love of Jesus, then our lives will display it. When we live as Jesus did, moving in compassion and mercy, advocating for those the world ridicules, we align our lives with his kingdom. May we live out our love loudly and plainly for all to see, leaving no one to wonder what our character is.

A FRIEND IN DEED

Choose to walk in the ways of Jesus
as you relate to others today.

LIVING STONES

You are living stones that God is building into his spiritual temple. What's more, you are his holy priests. Through the mediation of Jesus Christ, you offer spiritual sacrifices that please God.

1 Peter 2:5 nlt

As living stones being built by God, we are partakers and instruments of his kingdom. We are not only part of his kingdom, but we also have fellowship with the Creator. He places us where he sees fit, and we simply need to remain in him.

As you consider your friendships today, who would you say is built into your life? Who plays a major role in the makeup of your "house"? May you find encouragement that you are not isolated. Not one of us is meant to go it alone in life, and God has set us in his family of other living stones so together we build something stronger than we could have built on our own.

A FRIEND IN DEED

Thank the friends who are pillars in your life.

LOOK TO HIM

The LORD grants wisdom!
From his mouth come knowledge and understanding.

PROVERBS 2:6 NLT

Are you not sure of how to move forward in a friendship? Are you at a loss for what to do for a friend who is struggling? Do you want to go deeper in your understanding and care for others as well as being known by those you admire? First, look to the Lord. He grants wisdom when we are out of ideas. He gives clarity where we are confused. His Word is full of practical help to guide us in the right direction.

In the same way that we look to God for wisdom, may we rely on his wise counsel when we are offering advice to others. Let's encourage others in the mercy of God, and let's point them to his loving leadership. He never turns away an inquiring heart or a questioning mind!

A FRIEND IN DEED

Let your advice be rooted in the character and Word of God.

BUILD ON CHRIST

Let your roots grow down into him, and let your lives be built on him. Then your faith will grow strong in the truth you were taught, and you will overflow with thankfulness.

COLOSSIANS 2:7 NLT

When we build our lives upon the lovingkindness and truth of Christ, we are set on a firm foundation. Jesus said this himself in Matthew 7:24: "Anyone who listens to my teaching and follows it is wise, like a person who builds a house on solid rock." He goes on to say that though storms may come, the house won't collapse.

Are the houses of our lives built upon Christ's teachings? Are our relationships formed on the bedrock of his merciful truth? We cannot claim to simply believe in Christ without implementing his teaching in our lives. When we do, we are firmly established in his love. Even when the storms come, we will not collapse under their weight.

A FRIEND IN DEED

Apply a core teaching of Christ to your friendships and interactions today.

RAISED UP

> "He raises the poor from the dust and lifts the needy from the ash heap; he seats them with princes and has them inherit a throne of honor. For the foundations of the earth are the LORD's; on them he has set the world."

1 SAMUEL 2:8 NIV

Jesus is a wonderful Savior. He does not have a laundry list of things that we must do in order to be accepted by him. He does not "help those who help themselves," as we often hear misattributed to the Scriptures. The gospel of Christ is that he helps those who cannot help themselves. He intervenes in our neediness and lifts us up from the ashes.

When it comes to our relationships, do we approach them with the mentality of Christ or of popular society? If we refuse to help those in dire situations, to humanize those whom society degrades, and to excuse our lack of compassion with a trite reply, then we are not following in the footsteps of Christ. May we be challenged to love more, to judge less, and to move to the margins with compassion and humility.

A FRIEND IN DEED

Help a friend in need in a practical way.

GIFTS OF GRACE

By grace you have been saved through faith,
and that not of yourselves; it is the gift of God.

EPHESIANS 2:8 NKJV

Grace is a gift given freely. It is not earned, and it cannot be bartered. What God so liberally offers us, do we also offer to others? As recipients of generous mercy and grace that never ends, let's not grow stingy with our own measures of grace in the relationships we have.

If you struggle to offer grace to others, take that to the Lord and ask him to reveal why that is. If you do not see how you can give grace to yourself, this is also something to get curious about! The gift of grace is found in God. He can shine a light on the shadows of confusion or the lies that we believe about our own worthiness or that of others. Let's look to him first, spend time in prayer, and ask to be filled with fresh measures of his abounding grace!

A FRIEND IN DEED

*Ask the Lord for a fresh revelation of his grace in your life
and live with generosity from that place.*

JUST IMAGINE

Things never discovered or heard of before, things beyond
our ability to imagine—these are the many things God has
in store for all his lovers.

1 CORINTHIANS 2:9 TPT

There is greater knowledge, more vast understanding, and
more wonderful mechanisms at work in the world than we
have yet grasped. Science itself is constantly revealing the
intricacies of our universe. Why would we fall into the trap
of thinking we already know all there is to know?

Through the Holy Spirit, God reveals the mysteries of his
wisdom. The fullness of all that is will one day be revealed,
but none of us has the ability to grasp it now. May we look
to the Creator of all things, letting our imaginations grow
and expand in the wonders of his love! They cannot be
exaggerated. As we mature in our understanding, let us
apply heavenly imagination in the ways we relate to those
we love, building each other up in hope, faith, peace, joy,
and love.

A FRIEND IN DEED

*Let your imagination run wild
with how you can bless a friend today!*

CHOSEN TO SHARE

You are a chosen people, royal priests, a holy nation, a people for God's own possession. You were chosen to tell about the wonderful acts of God, who called you out of darkness into his wonderful light.

1 PETER 2:9 NCV

How often do you share about what God has done in your heart and life? Do the conversations you have with friends reflect the mercy of how the Lord has come through for you? If you have experienced a miracle, consider remembering it and sharing it with someone close to you today. If you have had a breakthrough by the grace of God, let it be a story you tell.

If you struggle to know how or what to share, instead of putting more pressure on yourself, consider asking a faithful friend to share a story of their own experience of God's faithfulness with you. It could be a practice in encouragement that fuels your own faith. Don't be ashamed to ask!

A FRIEND IN DEED

In a conversation with a friend, share a story of God's faithfulness or ask them to share one with you.

MARKED BY MERCY

Once you were not a people,
but now you are God's people;
once you had not received mercy,
but now you have received mercy.

1 PETER 2:10 ESV

Most of us who have followed the Lord for any length of time have a clear understanding of our lives before and after this decision. We may have had a remarkable conversion experience, or it may have been subtle. However, most of us have had growth in the revelation of God's mercy and what receiving that means for us. Our lives are transformed in the wonderful lovingkindness of our Savior's embrace.

Take some time to remember your own "before and after." How has the love of God enriched your life? How has it changed the way you relate to others? In going back to the beginning, perhaps you recognize areas where you can reinstate compassion, grace, patience, and mercy in your friendships. If so, take a step in that direction today.

A FRIEND IN DEED

Forgive an offense that you have been holding onto.

VESSELS OF HIS SPIRIT

What we have received is not the spirit of the world.
We have received the Spirit who is from God. The Spirit
helps us understand what God has freely given us.

1 CORINTHIANS 2:12 NIRV

The Spirit of God helps us understand what has been offered to us in Christ. What a wonderful and hopeful promise! All who know the Lord have been filled with his Spirit. When we enter into this fellowship, everything that God wants for us is available through him. We do not rely on our own strength but on his.

Do you feel a lack of connection with others? Do you struggle to know what is yours in Christ? Ask for help from the Spirit of God, and then ask for perspective from trusted believers. We cannot know what we cannot know, but we also will not grow if we do not seek the help of others: the Holy Spirit and our friends included!

A FRIEND IN DEED

*Ask for a friend's insight on a question
or decision you've been mulling over.*

TIME FOR SINGING

The flowers appear on the earth, the time of singing has come, and the voice of the turtledove is heard in our land.

SONG OF SOLOMON 2:12 ESV

Sometimes, the seasons of our lives do not align with the seasons of the earth. Though we may be in the dead of winter, perhaps our relationships and hope are thriving like the fruit of summer. Maybe we find ourselves in a time of letting go, like autumn, but a friend is experiencing the renewal of spring, where new life is popping up.

When the time of singing comes, it is a joy to share it with loved ones. Our shared gladness and celebration are as meaningful as our shared suffering and grief. Let's not shrink back from times of rejoicing with those we love for the new life that breaks through after the barrenness of winter. When flowers bloom, let's enjoy their scent and beauty.

A FRIEND IN DEED

Share a success with a friend or share in theirs!

EVEN WHEN

If we are not faithful, he will still be faithful,
because he must be true to who he is.

2 TIMOTHY 2:13 NCV

God's nature is unchanging. Even when we are completely
void of faith, walking our own path, God cannot go against
his character. He is still faithful! When we think about the
parable of the prodigal son, we can see that the mercy of the
Father never wavers no matter how far we wander!

Can we apply the same mercy we receive from the Father to
our own relationships? Even if others around us are letting
us down, can we continue to be faithful to what we know
is our part? Let's not let the actions of others keep us from
walking in integrity. And even when we fall, God is faithful;
he will help us right the wrongs we make along the way.
What a wonderful and predictably good Father he is!

A FRIEND IN DEED

*Let go of the guilt you have felt of failing to be perfect
in your relationships.*

BROUGHT NEAR

You have been united with Christ Jesus. Once you were far
away from God, but now you have been brought near to
him through the blood of Christ.

EPHESIANS 2:13 NLT

In the perfect unity we find in the Trinity, we discover
that connection is what we were created for. We have
been united with God through Christ and he does not
hold the errors of our ways against us. He welcomes us
into fellowship with Father, Son, and Spirit, with endless
love and kindness. May we find ourselves whole in him,
delighting in the communion we have.

Let's also remember that we were made to connect with
others. Through friendship, family (both inherited and
chosen), and community, we experience the goodness
of knowing and being known. Though our earthly
relationships are far from perfect or pain free, they can be
a greater glimpse into the glory of God. May we look for
where the light shines through our connection to others.

A FRIEND IN DEED

Make time to be with a friend in person today.

HEART WORK

God is working in you, giving you the desire and the power
to do what pleases him.

PHILIPPIANS 2:13 NLT

We may set our goals and work toward them, doing what
we know to achieve them, but even when we give our all,
perfection will never be possible. Perfection isn't the goal!
May we remember that staying connected to God and to
others is the way of the kingdom. The Lord leads us in love,
putting passion within our hearts and rekindling old flames
to keep us going. He is our help, and he is our perseverance.

Endless productivity is not godliness. Let's remember this
today! God is at work within our surrendered hearts even
when we cannot see or understand what he is doing. May
we remain yielded to his leadership, letting our best be
enough and letting his grace cover the rest. God is often at
work in the details that we overlook, so let's remain humble
and full of love and grace toward others.

A FRIEND IN DEED

*Give others grace today when they
don't meet your expectations.*

SWEET AROMAS

Thanks be to God, who always leads us as captives in
Christ's triumphal procession and uses us to spread the
aroma of the knowledge of him everywhere.

2 CORINTHIANS 2:14 NIV

We are partners in Christ, and we share in the inheritance
of his victory over death. We may be captive to Christ,
but we are liberated in his love! We share the spoils of his
triumph. That is complete freedom and fellowship with
the Father! He uses us to spread the sweet aroma of his
redeeming mercy.

Do you trust that God is working in your life as you remain
yielded to him? When you choose to follow in his footsteps,
letting love be the banner over your life and choices, the
sweet fragrance of your surrender and Christlikeness
becomes unmistakable. Continue to walk in the freedom
he has offered you and let his mercy be your source, your
inspiration, and your victory song.

A FRIEND IN DEED

*Show Christ's love to a friend today
with an intentional act of kindness.*

NO MORE WALLS

He himself is our peace, who has made us both one and has
broken down in his flesh the dividing wall of hostility.

EPHESIANS 2:14 ESV

In Christ, there is no excuse for hostility or volatility toward
others. He has become our peace, setting us right with God
the Father. He did what we could never do; he's given us
pure and confident fellowship with himself. What God does
not hold against us, may we not hold against others.

In Matthew 18, Jesus illustrates the hypocrisy of one who
has been shown mercy through the forgiveness of their
debt yet turns around and demands repayment from one
who owes him. When we refuse to forgive others from that
which we have been mercifully liberated, we erect walls of
hostility where Christ has offered peace. May we be people
who live generously, offering mercy and peace instead of
judgment and bitterness to others. When we have been
recipients of great kindness, it is only natural that we offer
kindness as well.

A FRIEND IN DEED

*Forgive a small debt that someone owes you
whether perceived or tangible.*

HIGH PRICE

He gave himself for us so he might pay the price to free us from all evil and to make us pure people who belong only to him—people who are always wanting to do good deeds.

TITUS 2:14 NCV

Jesus paid the highest price for our freedom, and not for us alone, but for everyone who comes to him. We cannot imagine how big and inclusive his mercy is. We cannot begin to fathom the depths of his grace! When we think we know, may we be quick to reframe our thoughts and imagine that being just the tip of the proverbial iceberg.

Christ has purified us; it is not something any of us could earn. May we approach our friendships with the same generosity of Christ. We are no better than anyone else. Our social or financial position does not make us smarter, more loveable, or more worthy of Christ's love than any other. May we keep from falling into the trap of comparison and see the beauty of every person, for Christ has created and offered everyone the same purity of purpose.

A FRIEND IN DEED

Let go of a bias you have held
and ask the Lord for compassion to replace it.

SWEET MESSAGES

The Messiah has come to preach
this sweet message of peace to you,
the ones who were distant,
and to those who are near.

EPHESIANS 2:17 TPT

Do you feel like the Gospel requires too much of you? Let this be your challenge: go back to the source today. Ask the Holy Spirit to reveal the heart of the Father, the truth of Jesus, and the comfort of his presence as you read through the teachings of Christ today. Don't let what you have been told to believe set the tone. Look to the source.

The Holy Spirit offers revelation to those who ask. Look in the Word and read what Jesus actually displayed through his words and life. Let your curiosity lead you to ask questions; he welcomes your thoughts, your wonderings, and your doubts. You are not too much to handle. As you receive his help, let the peace he offers be extended in every interaction you have.

A FRIEND IN DEED

*Let peace be the thing you offer yourself,
your friends, and strangers today.*

HELP FOR US

He himself suffered when he was tempted.
Now he is able to help others who are being tempted.

HEBREWS 2:18 NIRV

When you think of Jesus, do you imagine that he never felt tired, crabby, or sad? We often imagine him as superhuman which is not entirely true. Though he was the Son of God, he was also fully human. This means he disappointed people, felt grief, and had to learn how to participate in society.

We know that Jesus was tempted. This is no secret. When he was tempted, he used the Word of God and the help of the Spirit to overcome. He came out of his desert season exhausted but victorious. Instead of turning away from God in our time of need and temptation, let's turn to him for help. He is not surprised by our weakness; Jesus knows it well for he had to deal with the limits of humanity himself.

A FRIEND IN DEED

*When a friend shares a struggle with temptation,
turn toward them rather than away.*

ALIVE IN CHRIST

My old self has been crucified with Christ. It is no longer I who live, but Christ lives in me. So I live in this earthly body by trusting in the Son of God, who loved me and gave himself for me.

GALATIANS 2:20 NLT

The power of Christ is available to all who believe and have submitted to his leadership. The power of Christ makes the lame walk, the deaf hear, and the blind see. He gives revelation to the searching heart, peace to those riddled with anxiety, and endless mercy for restoration.

As we come alive in Christ, so will our relationships. Instead of isolating ourselves and seeking our own advantages, we will reach out with generous grace to those around us. Everything and everyone benefits from the life of Christ within us! May we press into the life and freedom we have, here and now, all while offering the liberating love we receive to our friends, family, and communities.

A FRIEND IN DEED

*Trust God to do what you cannot,
and let his faithfulness be where your expectations lie.*

MARCH

Encourage each other
and build each other up,
just as you are already doing.

1 Thessalonians 5:11 nlt

WONDERFUL THINGS

"He reveals deep and secret things;
He knows what is in the darkness,
and light dwells with Him."

DANIEL 2:22 NKJV

Nothing is hidden from God. He sees everything clearly, from the beginning of time until the end of its borders. He is not surprised by the things that take us off guard. He is steadfast in loyal love, and we can find our feet on the bedrock of his sufficiency. Let's lean into him with hearts that trust, even as he reveals what is on his heart today.

It is wonderful to fellowship with our Creator: to share our hearts, lives, and dreams with one who knows and cares about us. Let's not neglect the relationships in our lives where that is true as well. Communion and intimacy are gifts that reflect God. We were made to come alive in the context of relationship! When was the last time you revealed a deep and secret thing to a close and trusted friend?

A FRIEND IN DEED

Share what's on your heart with a friend today.

SIGNS OF HOPE

Rejoice, you people of Jerusalem!
Rejoice in the LORD your God!
For the rain he sends demonstrates his faithfulness.
Once more the autumn rains will come,
as well as the rains of spring.

JOEL 2:23 NLT

The cycles of nature point us to the hand of our Creator. The rains that water the earth reflect the provision of the Father. The bees that pollinate the flowers show the cycles of renewal within the earth. If you have been through a winter of the soul, then you know what it is to look for signs of life.

May the wonders of creation remind you of the faithfulness of your Father. Take some time to consider the activity going on outside and ask the Lord to show you what it reflects about him. There are signs of hope if you look for them. Let the promises of God fill your heart with encouragement and hope.

A FRIEND IN DEED

Share what the Lord has shown you with a friend.

SEASONS OF LIFE

The threshing floors will again be piled high with grain, and the presses will overflow with new wine and olive oil.

JOEL 2:24 NLT

Today, let's take the idea of seasons within nature and apply it even more readily to our lives. Think about the characteristics of the season you have been in. Has it felt barren? Have you struggled through it? You may find that you have been in a winter. Have you felt nostalgia and grief in needing to let go? Have you been in a long transition? Perhaps you have been in an autumn.

Maybe you have been breezing through, full of energy, play, hope, and life; perhaps you have been in a summer of sorts. Or maybe you are on the cusp of something new, seeing the buds of new life breaking open, entering a glorious new spring. Whatever season you are or have been in, consider the traits and the growth, the beauty and the characteristics that are also present there. And remember, our lives are cyclical just like nature. *The threshing floors will again be piled with grain.*

A FRIEND IN DEED

Ask a friend what kind of season they have been in.

SPIRIT TRUTH

His anointing teaches you about everything, and is true,
and is no lie—just as it has taught you, abide in him.

1 JOHN 2:27 ESV

In the context of this Scripture, we can understand the
anointing that John speaks of as the Holy Spirit who is
poured into us. Through the anointing of his presence, he
places illumination, wisdom, and the fruit of his life within
us. He is our ready and able teacher in all things.

What do you do when you are struggling to find your way?
Who do you turn to when you don't know what to do? The
Holy Spirit is always available. He often works within our
hearts, bringing revelation and clarity. He can do this when
we are alone, or he can do it through others. You don't have
to figure it out on your own. Ask for advice from those you
know and trust. The Holy Spirit can move powerfully within
you as they speak and give you discernment for your way.

A FRIEND IN DEED

*Ask a friend for their input on a matter
but pay attention to the Spirit moving in your heart.*

WATERFALLS OF GRACE

"I will pour out my spirit on all flesh; your sons and your daughters shall prophesy, your old men shall dream dreams, and your young men shall see visions."

JOEL 2:28 NRSV

No one is excluded from the gifts and anointing of God's Spirit. The young and the old and everyone in between have a place in his kingdom and have access to his wisdom. How diverse are our relationships? Do we have friends of all ages? Hopefully, we do not only rely on the people our own age. There is joy and wonder in youth, and there is wisdom and grace in age.

May you find your heart open to conversations with people no matter their age, race, class, or distinction. Don't be afraid to reach outside of your own identity and really listen with an open heart and mind. God is not only found in the places of our comfort zones. He is with all people, reaching out and using those who look to him. May we look for marks of his mercy already at work in those outside our spheres.

A FRIEND IN DEED

Have a conversation with someone different than you today, without any agenda but to listen.

CHILDREN OF GOD

See what kind of love the Father has given to us,
that we should be called children of God; and so we are.
The reason why the world does not know us
is that it did not know him.

1 JOHN 3:1 ESV

The love of the Father is wonderful. He has lavished his deep mercy upon us, drawn us into his family, and called us his very own children. What a gift! Our Father's identity has now become our own. His name marks us, and we are known as his heirs and his beloved. He is the perfect father, never punishing in anger or pulling away in pride. He is full of loyal love forever.

Let us find our true identity as children of God. When we could become discouraged by the actions and words of others when they tear us down, let's instead remain rooted and grounded in his love. May we never give up reflecting his mercy in our lives by choosing to be like him. He is worth it!

A FRIEND IN DEED

*Let go of an offense against someone
who refuses to understand you.*

GENEROUS KINDNESS

"How are you any different from others
if you limit your kindness only to your friends?
Don't even the ungodly do that?"

MATTHEW 5:47 TPT

Jesus points out to his followers that it is not exceptional to love those who already love you. It is not out of the ordinary to be kind to those we know, trust, and support. The call to love as Christ loves is much broader than this. It is to be gracious to those we disagree with, to show kindness to those who don't like us, and to be loving to those who are self-absorbed.

This is no small task. We must remember that we don't love from a place of lack. We don't only give to those who have poured into us. Generosity does not require an exchange. God is love, and he gives freely because it is who he is. What if we moved from seeing love less as an act of sacrifice and more as an identity from which we live? How would that change the way we interact with others?

A FRIEND IN DEED

Be kind regardless of others' attitudes today.

EMPOWERED BY GOD

We don't see ourselves as capable enough to do anything in our own strength, for our true competence flows from God's empowering presence.

2 CORINTHIANS 3:5 TPT

It is an eventuality, a fact of life really, that we will grow tired of being gracious. Our self-preserving boundaries will grow weak and penetrable, making us irritable. It is not a sin to be weak. May we let ourselves off the hook when our humanity shows up in full form. Instead of letting shame sweep over us and cause us to overreact, let's lean into the grace of God.

When we rely on God to empower us, there is mercy to restore, grace to rebuild, and kindness to refresh our weary souls. Let's not overlook the importance of time away from stimuli that could send us over the edge. May we lean on the power of God's Spirit to help us, even and especially in our relationships. He gives us the grace to seek restoration with those we love in humility and transparency.

A FRIEND IN DEED

When you mess up today, turn to God
and seek restoration with those affected.

BETTER UNDERSTANDING

May the Lord lead your hearts into a full understanding
and expression of the love of God and the patient
endurance that comes from Christ.

2 Thessalonians 3:5 NLT

Don't we want the best for those we love? Whether it's a
partner, a friend, or a child, we want them to thrive in
their God-given opportunities. We want them to flourish
as they were always created to do. May we be vocal in our
encouragement today, praying for each of these precious
people and sharing our hopes with them.

Above all, may we intercede for the character of God to be
revealed to our loved ones. May they be drawn into a fuller
understanding of his love, knowing how wide and plentiful
it is! May they know without a doubt that they cannot
escape the love of God. May we champion their wisdom
and freedom without the need to manage how that looks
or what they decide. We are each our own, but we are also
witnesses and support for one another.

A FRIEND IN DEED

*Pray for a loved one and share with them
how much you are championing their growth!*

RENEWED

He saved us, not on the basis of deeds which we have done in righteousness, but according to His mercy, by the washing of regeneration and renewing by the Holy Spirit.

TITUS 3:5 NASB

Renewal in the Spirit comes not when we have earned it, but when we have turned to him and received his life. He does the work of cultivating the seeds that have already been sown in the soil of our hearts. He waters them with the lifegiving power of his words, and he shines on us with the radiant light of his presence.

Is there a friend who has been fighting their way through the darkness of grief, pain, suffering, or loss? Pray for renewal to come through the Spirit's work in their heart and life. Reach out with words of loving encouragement and affirmation but refrain from giving advice. Let the Lord's work in them be enough, and love them where they are at, holding onto the hope of their season of spring that is coming.

A FRIEND IN DEED

Buy flowers for a friend who has been struggling.

KEEP SEEKING

Seek his will in all you do,
and he will show you which path to take.

PROVERBS 3:6 NLT

When we walk with the Lord, looking to his leadership and allowing his grace to direct us, we need not fear taking a wrong path. Even if we take steps one way, he can redirect us with his love. His will is not a tightrope to master; we don't have to worry about perfection. Life is like a dance, and he is our dance partner. Let's remain focused on him, and he will guide us through the dance.

It is not easy to disappoint God. He is not surprised by us, and he sees us through the lens of his love. May we offer others the same grace that he offers us in relationship to him. Are we easily disappointed and frustrated by others? Perhaps it has less to do with them and more to do with our expectations. Instead of letting disappointment lead you today, let curiosity and grace guide you to the throne of God where you can fill up on his mercy and offer it others.

A FRIEND IN DEED

Get clear about your expectations in friendships.

WHAT JOY

How can we thank God enough for you in return for all the
joy we have in the presence of our God because of you?

1 THESSALONIANS 3:9 NIV

We all need friends who lift us from our foul moods and
distract us from the overwhelming tasks of life. We also
need friends who will allow us to be real with where we
are, while encouraging us that there is more. There is joy in
intimate relationship. There is joy in support. There is joy in
celebration and fun. There is joy in true friendship.

Who are the friends you can rely on to show up for you?
Who shows up with food and drinks when you cannot
cook, plays with your children, or walks your dog with you?
Who will whisk you away from your troubles if only for an
hour or two? Give thanks for them today!

A FRIEND IN DEED

*Write a thank you card to a dear friend
for their reliability and support.*

RIGHT ON TIME

The Lord is not slow in doing what he promised—the way some people understand slowness. But God is being patient with you. He does not want anyone to be lost, but he wants all people to change their hearts and lives.

2 PETER 3:9 NCV

God is wise and patient, not moving too quickly or too slowly. When we feel as if we have missed our chance, whether in life or in our relationships, may we remember that God is a redeemer, and he works everything out for the good of those who love him. Let's trust that his mercy is powerful enough to transform our lives; he takes our willingness and couples it with his power.

If we have been slow in following through on something for a friend, let's take the opportunity this day affords to move ahead with it. It is not too late to put in the effort. Let's not let discouragement or fear keep us from doing what we know to do! God is our strength, and he will help us. Today is the only time we have, so let's embrace it!

A FRIEND IN DEED

Follow through on something you said you would do.

BEAUTIFULLY CULTIVATED

God has made everything beautiful for its own time.
He has planted eternity in the human heart,
but even so, people cannot see the whole scope
of God's work from beginning to end.

ECCLESIASTES 3:11 NLT

God himself has planted eternity within our hearts. Loss and grief are painful. They feel unnatural, as if they weren't what we were created for. Goodbyes speak of the limits of time and humanity. In the eternal kingdom of Christ, there will be no end! When we feel the ache of eternity pulling our hearts, may we remember that though time on this earth is fleeting, there is more to come than we can imagine.

This is not to say that our lives on the earth are meaningless. Far from it! May we learn to embrace the present moment and the simple joys of fellowship with one another. Let's give thanks for what and who we have in our lives right here and now. Let's lean into the beauties and complexities of friendship!

A FRIEND IN DEED

*Be present in your conversations today
and treat this day as if it's the only day that matters.*

OVERFLOWING LOVE

May the Lord make your love for one another
and for all people grow and overflow.

1 Thessalonians 3:12 NLT

To love one another is the second greatest commandment
that Jesus gave us. He told his disciples in John 13:34, as
his capture and death were approaching, "I am giving you
a new commandment: Love each other. Just as I have loved
you, you should love each other." Just as Christ has loved us,
that's how we should love others.

Is the standard of our love for friends, neighbors,
coworkers, and family that which is revealed in the status
quo or as evidenced in the love of Christ? They are vastly
different ideals! We are to love others with humility and
grace, kindness and honesty. We champion the underdog
and show compassion to those the world despises. We
offer forgiveness to our enemies and let go of our rights to
comfort. This is how others will know that we are actually
disciples of Christ: by our lived-out love!

A FRIEND IN DEED

Go out of your way to be extravagant with kindness today.

DRESSED IN COMPASSION

Put on then, as God's chosen ones, holy and beloved,
compassionate hearts, kindness, humility, meekness,
and patience.

COLOSSIANS 3:12 ESV

When we live as reflections of Christ's love, it is only natural
that we clothe ourselves with his compassion, cultivate
kindness in our hearts, remain humble and teachable, be
pliable in his grace, and grow patient in the journey of life.
None of this happens by accident; we are transformed by
the love of God as we fellowship with him in Spirit and in
truth, yielding our lives to him.

Take some time to pray this verse over yourself and over
your interactions today. May you be clothed in compassion,
ready with kindness, and remain humble in the mercy of
Christ. As you go about your day, may you remember this
mandate and know that the Spirit is your strength and help.
Rely on him, and he will help you.

A FRIEND IN DEED

*Pray for greater compassion and recognize where
you see it in your conversations and interactions.*

CONFIDENT TRUST

In him and through faith in him we may approach God
with freedom and confidence.

EPHESIANS 3:12 NIV

We are drawn into the heart of Christ with his relentless
kindness. We are brought to repentance with his tender
love that beckons us to lay down our worn-out ways. We
know when we are simply spinning our wheels. Though
we may want our own way, true freedom comes in the love
of Christ where we are liberated to choose from a place of
confident trust rather than dreaded obligation.

How freely can your friends approach you? Are you a
trustworthy and compassionate presence? May you be a
place of safety and security, support, and compassion for
those in your life. May you be steadfast and secure in the
love of God, knowing that you can offer that same kind of
liberating mercy to others. There is no shortage of grace in
the heart of God, and we need never operate on our own
resources when he is our true source and never-ending
supply.

A FRIEND IN DEED

*Offer your unconditional love to a friend no matter
whether you agree or disagree with their choices.*

LEAVE ROOM

Make allowance for each other's faults,
and forgive anyone who offends you.
Remember, the Lord forgave you,
so you must forgive others.

COLOSSIANS 3:13 NLT

None of us is perfect, and it is simply an eventuality that we will let others down—even those we love dearly. Instead of holding ourselves and others to an impossible standard, let's leave room for faults, forgiving the offenses of friends and being humble in seeking restoration for our own.

The Lord has forgiven us of all our sins, so let's not withhold our forgiveness from those in our own lives. Especially when it comes to our loved ones, let's be liberal with love and relentless with forgiveness! Let's move in wisdom, knowing when to simply let go and move on and when to confront the matter. The Holy Spirit is our help even in this!

A FRIEND IN DEED

Refrain from micromanaging a loved one's actions today.

FOCUSED

I don't depend on my own strength to accomplish this;
however I do have one compelling focus: I forget all of the
past as I fasten my heart to the future instead.

PHILIPPIANS 3:13 TPT

When we are overly focused on the past, we can get caught
up in regret or in romanticizing days gone by. It is a good
practice to remember where we have already journeyed
especially in our relationship with the Lord. But when we
ruminate on what we cannot change, it can take us into
spirals of shame.

Let's let go of what we cannot control and instead look
ahead to what we can create with the time we have. Let's
work on building our relationships and homes with love,
purpose, and grace. Let's focus on the possibilities that lie
ahead and what we can do to move toward them today.

*Think about what you want your friendships to look like
and make a move to strengthen them today.*

PEACEFUL POSSIBILITIES

May the Lord of peace himself give you peace
at all times in every way.

2 THESSALONIANS 3:16 ESV

What a prayer this is that Paul speaks over the Thessalonian church! *May the Lord…give you peace at all times in every way.* Not sometimes, in some ways, but *at all times in every way.* Are we promoters of peace in our relationships? Do we look for ways to make the lives of our friends and family more peaceful?

What is one small thing you can do today for a loved one that you know will add to their peace of mind or peace of heart? Perhaps dropping off a meal for a friend will allow them to release the work of having to figure out what to make. Maybe you know that a clean kitchen adds to your significant other's peace of mind. Whatever you do, look for ways to promote peace for someone you care about today and let it be your gift to them.

A FRIEND IN DEED

Create a peaceful atmosphere with your loved ones.

BREATH OF GOD

Every Scripture has been written by the Holy Spirit, the breath of God. It will empower you by its instruction and correction, giving you the strength to take the right direction and lead you deeper into the path of godliness.

2 TIMOTHY 3:16 TPT

Have you ever known the encouragement, relief, or comfort of an aptly spoken word? Perhaps it was a Scripture verse or a note from a friend. The Word of God is full of encouragement for our souls, lessons for our maturity, and reflections of God's character.

Proverbs 16:24 says, "Nothing is more appealing than speaking beautiful, lifegiving words, for they release sweetness to our souls and inner healing to our spirits." When was the last time you reached out to friend with beautiful, lifegiving words? Take some time in prayer, asking the Lord to highlight someone you could share a word of hope with. Pray for them, letting his Spirit guide you.

A FRIEND IN DEED

Share a verse and word of encouragement with a friend.

DWELLING IN WISDOM

Let the word of Christ dwell in you richly, teaching and admonishing one another in all wisdom, singing Psalms and hymns and spiritual songs, with thankfulness in your hearts to God.

COLOSSIANS 3:16 ESV

How often do you let the Word of God go deeper than a quick reading? When we meditate on Scripture, we allow it to reach beyond our intellect into the application of it in our lives. We let it challenge, teach, and direct us.

May we only offer to others what we have already submitted ourselves to. Let's not offer wisdom to others that we refuse to back up with our actions. Let's be people of integrity and honor, encouraging others in compassion and humility. The place of change always starts in us. May we focus on what we can do to grow in the wisdom of Christ's kingdom and live it out.

A FRIEND IN DEED

*Let what you offer to others be encouraging to them
in their own walk with the Lord.*

FREEDOM IS HERE

The Lord is the Spirit,
and wherever the Spirit of the Lord is,
there is freedom.

2 CORINTHIANS 3:17 NLT

Are there any friendships you have where you do not feel the freedom to be yourself? If so, consider what is at the root of it. Is it your assumption of what the other friend will find acceptable? Is there a lack of vulnerability or safety in the relationship? If you have not ventured to be vulnerable with that friend, consider whether you want to try and deepen that friendship or accept it the way it is.

The Spirit of God gives us freedom to live as confident children of the Father. We do not need to conform to the expectations or will of others. We are free to be ourselves, to love God and others, and to choose our close friends and confidants. Let's be intentional with our freedom!

A FRIEND IN DEED

*Show up as you are, not how you think others
want you to be, in your friendships today.*

ALL FOR JESUS

Whatever you do in word or deed, do all in the name of the Lord Jesus, giving thanks through Him to God the Father.

COLOSSIANS 3:17 NASB

When we focus on what people around us expect, we can become burnt out and resentful that we are being stretched thin. Instead of complaining or grumbling to ourselves while doing chores around the house, going out of our way to meet a friend, or doing a task that we wish others would do, let's approach it as if we were doing it for God. He sees what others miss.

If there is a conversation to be had about boundaries or expectations, by all means have it, but be clear and not accusatory. If things still need to be done, whether or not someone else can step in, let them off the hook and release bitterness from your heart as you do it unto the Lord. Offer your words and deeds as a sacrifice of praise today!

A FRIEND IN DEED

Do the dishes for those who live with you as an act of service.

SAVED BY MERCY

"God did not send his Son into the world to judge the
world guilty, but to save the world through him."

JOHN 3:17 NCV

Read the verse for today again. *God did not send his Son…to
judge the world guilty.* How often do our hearts lean toward
judgment? How often do we look for ways to excuse our
desire for vengeance? We are human, and in our humanity,
we want things to feel, look, and be fair. This world does
not work that way though. Christ came to set us free from
the chains of sin and death. He calls us to a new standard:
one that offers mercy instead of judgment.

Are we quick to show understanding to those we love?
Do we offer them mercy and grace instead of pointed
judgment or the desire for them to conform to our ideals?
We cannot control our friends or family. We cannot dictate
their choices. God does not do this to us either. He gives us
freedom to choose how we will live, and he offers us mercy.
May we offer the same to those around us!

A FRIEND IN DEED

*When a friend confides in you, resist the urge
to direct them with your opinions.*

IN OUR MIDST

The LORD your God is in your midst,
a mighty one who will save;
he will rejoice over you with gladness;
he will quiet you by his love;
he will exult over you with loud singing.

ZEPHANIAH 3:17 ESV

When we are overwhelmed by life, worried by the unknowns that we cannot predict, may we put our trust in Emmanuel—God with us! He is in our midst, as this Scripture proclaims. He rejoices over us with gladness. He quiets us with his love.

When our friends are going through dark and unsettled times, may we walk with them in the same way the Lord walks with us. May we be a source of comfort and relief. May our love help quiet their fears as we steadfastly support them through their trouble. A faithful friend is a gift.

A FRIEND IN DEED

*Reach out to a friend who is grieving
with a tangible act of love.*

CONTINUALLY TRANSFORMED

We all, with unveiled face, beholding the glory of the Lord,
are being transformed into the same image from one degree
of glory to another. For this comes from the Lord who is
the Spirit.

2 CORINTHIANS 3:18 ESV

Life does not lend to us being stagnant, neither in our
faith nor in our living situations. May we embrace the
opportunities to change when they arise. May we continue
to cultivate our souls, our relationships with God and
others, and our faith as we embrace the transformation of
God's Spirit along the way.

Do we also embrace the changes our friends go through, or
do we resist them? We will all continue to evolve through
our circumstances and choices, and our relationships will
have to as well. Instead of wishing that things would remain
the same, let's look for ways to support each other in the
new phases of our lives.

A FRIEND IN DEED

*Celebrate a friend's transformation
even if it is something you have to adjust to.*

GOD IS GREATER

This is how we know that we belong to the truth and how we set our hearts at rest in his presence: If our hearts condemn us, we know that God is greater than our hearts, and he knows everything.

1 JOHN 3:19 NIV

God is greater than us! Hallelujah! That is very good news. He knows everything; nothing is hidden from him. Nothing can surprise him either. He is greater than our intentions, our understandings, and our greatest failures. He cannot be taken off guard, for he sees every possibility clearly.

Do we trust that God can handle our mess? Do we trust that he can do the same for our friends and family? May we find rest in his presence today and trust him to do what only he can do in our hearts and lives. He can do far more than we can imagine, and he can do it much better than we ever could.

A FRIEND IN DEED

Pray for a friend and trust God to work out his redemption and restoration for them.

SURE STEPS

The Sovereign LORD is my strength! He makes me as
surefooted as a deer, able to tread upon the heights.

HABAKKUK 3:19 NLT

This verse in Habakkuk echoes the sentiment in Proverbs
3:6, "Become intimate with him in whatever you do, and
he will lead you wherever you go" (TPT). The Lord is
our strength, and he is our faithful leader. He makes our
feet stable, and he shows us the way to go, whether to the
heights of the mountains or the depths of the valleys.

Even when we forget how faithful God is, he does not
change. He loyally leads us, empowers us with his Spirit,
and works his redemptive love through our lives. May we
remember that he is able to strengthen our resolve and
make us able to scale the heights to which he is calling us.
Let's ask for his perspective over our lives as well as his
thread of faithfulness over the lives of our friends!

A FRIEND IN DEED

Encourage a friend by sharing today's verse with them.

OUT OF DARKNESS

"Behold, at that time I will deal with all your oppressors.
And I will save the lame and gather the outcast, and I will
change their shame into praise and renown in all the earth."

ZEPHANIAH 3:19 ESV

When we partner with the power of God's love in our lives,
we choose to align ourselves with his kingdom and its ways.
He gives beauty for ashes, mercy in place of judgment, aid
to the vulnerable and the outcast, and help to those in need.
Do our lives reflect these principles of Christ's kingdom?

May we do much more than simply show mercy to those
with whom we are comfortable. May we show mercy
to those we struggle to get along with, those we cannot
understand and whose lives we would never choose to
lead. May we clothe ourselves in the compassion of Christ
that gathers the outcast, gives honor in place of shame, and
dignifies those who are belittled by society. In doing so, we
become arbiters of God's great grace.

A FRIEND IN DEED

Help someone in need today.

HEAVENLY HOME

Our homeland is in heaven, and we are waiting for our
Savior, the Lord Jesus Christ, to come from heaven.

PHILIPPIANS 3:20 NCV

We are sojourners in the earth; we are only passing
through. This is true of every life. May we not use our faith
in God to make pride-filled distinctions that separate our
worth from the worth of others. Every life is worthy of
honor, respect, and love. As we live seeking to honor God,
we cannot escape the call to love others well.

We catch glimpses of what home feels like in this life: a
warm meal shared with loved ones, a fire roaring on a
cold day, the safety of community, knowing others and
being known, a warm hug, the relief and excitement of
connection. As we wait for our heavenly home, may we not
overlook the glimpses of home we have here and now.

A FRIEND IN DEED

Look for ways to extend hospitality today.

APRIL

Make allowance for each other's
faults, and forgive anyone who
offends you. Remember,
the Lord forgave you,
so you must forgive others.

COLOSSIANS 3:13 NLT

LISTEN FOR THE KNOCK

"Listen! I am standing at the door, knocking;
if you hear my voice and open the door,
I will come in to you and eat with you, and you with me."

REVELATION 3:20 NRSV

Jesus stands and knocks. When we hear him and open the door of our hearts to him, he enters in by his Spirit. He fellowships with us, and we commune with him. There is nothing that keeps us from his presence. We have only to open our hearts to him, and he will make himself at home there.

If you know the wonderful fellowship of the Spirit, having yielded your life to Jesus Christ, then live in the freedom of his love today. Share your hope with someone who is struggling. Remind a friend just how good God has been and always will be. Share your testimony of his goodness. If you have not opened the door to your heart to Christ, answer his call today and welcome him in. He will astound you with his mercy!

A FRIEND IN DEED

Share a testimony of God's faithfulness with a friend.

SO MUCH MORE

With God's power working in us, God can do much, much more than anything we can ask or imagine.

EPHESIANS 3:21 NCV

The power that Paul is speaking of in this verse is the power of God. It is the same power that resurrected Christ from the grave and transformed him once and for all, breaking the curse of sin and death. Christ's resurrection is the hope of our own!

As you spend time in the presence of God today, let your prayers grow bolder and bigger. Believe in God's power; believe that he can do much more than anything you could imagine. Press in and dream bigger, ultimately praying that God would have his way and move in mighty mercy. We can trust him to do far greater things than we could ask or envision even when we don't understand the path that takes us there.

A FRIEND IN DEED

Pray for God to work his power in your friends' lives.

WHOLEHEARTED RELIANCE

Trust in the Lord completely,
and do not rely on your own opinions.
With all your heart rely on him to guide you,
and he will lead you in every decision you make.

PROVERBS 3:5 TPT

When we trust in the Lord to guide us, we can let go of the need to do things perfectly. He takes even our missteps and leads us back onto the path of his mercy. We don't have to worry about going to the right or to the left when we look to the Lord as our leader. Sometimes he will be clear, and other times he will leave the choice to us. Either way, he will never leave us to walk the path of life alone.

Do you worry about your friends and their choices? Do you wonder if they will wander so far from what is right that God would not find them? Remember who God is and promises to be. Trust that just as he guides you, he will also lead everyone who looks to him, and it is never too late for a fresh start in his mercy.

A FRIEND IN DEED

*Trust God's work in your friends' lives
and love them as they are.*

SUFFICIENT PORTION

"The LORD is my portion," says my soul,
"therefore I will hope in him."

LAMENTATIONS 3:24 ESV

What does it do to your heart when you consider that
the Lord is your portion? Does it feel like it is not quite
enough? Does it feel too esoteric and not practical enough?
Perhaps it speaks of your experience: when you didn't know
how you would get through a dismal day, the Spirit of the
Lord filled you with love, peace, hope, and strength that
was not your own.

However weak you are feeling today, the Lord has
generous grace for you. He will help you not only in your
circumstances, but also in your relationships. Lean into
his grace, for his strength will be made perfect in your
surrendered weakness.

A FRIEND IN DEED

Ask God for grace to deal with difficult interactions today.

PEACEFUL REST

When you lie down, you will not be afraid;
when you lie down, your sleep will be sweet.

PROVERBS 3:24 NIV

Have you ever lost sleep because of anxiety? In this day and age, it's hard to find someone who hasn't. God doesn't promise us that we will escape hard circumstances, but he does promise to be with us, to fight for us, and to keep us in his perfect peace.

Ask the Lord to reveal the worries that have been keeping you from true rest. How many of them are based in relationships? Can you give your worries to God and ask him to fill your heart with peace, rest, and trust? He cares for you like a loving father, and he will do what you could never do on your own. Let go and rest in his peace. Go to sleep tonight with prayers of release, trusting that God will help you.

A FRIEND IN DEED

*Release your relationship anxieties
to the Lord in prayer tonight.*

NO MATTER WHAT

God is your confidence in times of crisis,
keeping your heart at rest in every situation.

PROVERBS 3:26 TPT

It can be hard to watch our friends walk through difficult times especially when the crisis is drawn out and painful. May we be better than fair-weather friends who disappear when the going gets tough. When our friends are suffering, may we be reliable places of support. May we offer encouragement and love, no matter how long their dark night lasts. May we show up in ways that we can and give up on trying to do it perfectly.

Who do you look to with confidence in your times of need, knowing their support will be there no matter what? God is the only perfect help, but we also have support available to us in our close relationships. May we take hope and encouragement in Christ's faithful love, his unending support, and his never-yielding presence.

A FRIEND IN DEED

Thank a friend who has proven to be a support in a crisis.

HEALING IS COMING

For you who fear my name,
the sun of righteousness shall rise
with healing in its wings.

MALACHI 4:2 ESV

If our lives are yielded to the leadership of Christ, we have a greater hope awaiting us in the revelation and reality of his coming kingdom. Even if we suffer now, we will not suffer in his kingdom. Even if we have pain now, we will be healed forever in the light of his presence as we dwell with him in eternity.

Some of us will experience the miracle of healing in our lives here and now. Others will only know the relief of the fullness of life when we are dwelling in the kingdom of Christ after our souls have crossed over from this life to the next. Either way, healing is coming. The son of righteousness *will* rise with healing in his wings. What a glorious hope to look forward to.

A FRIEND IN DEED

Share your hope for eternity with a friend.

OVERCOMERS

You, dear children, are from God and have overcome them,
because the one who is in you is greater than the one who
is in the world.

1 John 4:4 NIV

In the revelation of Christ as the Son of God, there is
freedom to overcome the ideologies and teachings that
reject him. We know that God is love because Christ made
it so very clear that he is. We know that we can face any
challenge because the Spirit of God is in us. He empowers
us to overcome, and it is always by love that we do so.

Look to the life and teachings of Jesus and you will find
wisdom to walk in. There is freedom for the captive, health
for the sick, and understanding for those who are lacking
it. Whatever challenges you face today, Christ is the way
to overcome. Whatever challenges your friends face, this
is true for them too. Press on in the presence of God and
lean into his present grace, for he will be your strength and
courage.

A FRIEND IN DEED

*Look to Jesus for truth, encouragement,
and hope for your relationships.*

RECEIVE WITH THANKS

Everything God made is good,
and nothing should be refused
if it is accepted with thanks.

1 TIMOTHY 4:4 NCV

How many of us have put ourselves on a restrictive diet of some sort? Likely most have. When we restrict ourselves from eating certain things, we do it in the hope of health. But what is off-limits for us is not necessarily for someone else. Do we judge others based on what they eat or don't eat? Paul was clear that there is freedom for all in Christ. If we are not condemned by what we put in our bodies, then we can receive his blessings with hearts full of thanks.

When you gather with friends over a meal, do not compare what you choose to eat with what others do. There is no one-size-fits-all model of health. If you were allergic to something, you would not eat it knowingly because of its effects. Whatever you or your friends eat, let it be a judgment-free experience. Paul was clear that morality does not lie in our food choices, so let's not fall into that trap ourselves!

A FRIEND IN DEED

Enjoy a meal with a friend.

TODAY'S JOYS

Rejoice in the Lord always.
I will say it again: Rejoice!

PHILIPPIANS 4:4 NIV

Every day affords new opportunities to experience the grace and mercy of the Lord. Look outside. Are there birds chirping? Does the sun shine, or is there rain watering the thirsty ground? May you look with expectancy for signs of spring and feel the joys of a new season as you recognize the emergence of life all around.

Life does not have to be perfect or pain free to be meaningful. There is air to breathe, candles to light, dogs to walk, birds to watch, and so much more. What simple things add joy to your day? How can you cultivate a practice of gratitude and expansion by leaning into these things more? Rejoice in the pleasures that are yours today. Rejoice in the presence of the Lord with you. Rejoice in a new day. Rejoice for the sake of rejoicing. Simply rejoice.

A FRIEND IN DEED

Share the simple joys you discover today with a friend.

CONFIDENT CHILDREN

Because you are his sons,
God sent the Spirit of his Son into our hearts,
the Spirit who calls out, "Abba, Father."

GALATIANS 4:6 NIV

As beloved children, we learn that we can come to our parents without fear of being shamed or ignored. Even if our natural family did not allow for this type of confident freedom, we have a perfect and loving heavenly Father who welcomes us whenever we come to him. We can approach without fear, knowing how dearly loved we are.

Whenever we need our Father, he is near. When we call out to him, he hears us, answers us, and holds us close. We can trust that when we ask him for help, he will always move in faithfulness. His ways are far better than our own, so let's trust his loyal love more than our dictations of happiness. He can handle us no matter what state we are in, so let's freely and confidently come to him with everything in our lives!

A FRIEND IN DEED

Encourage a brother or sister in Christ by reminding them of the affection of their heavenly Father.

CONTINUE IN LOVE

Dear friends, let us continue to love one another,
for love comes from God. Anyone who loves is a child
of God and knows God.

1 JOHN 4:7 NLT

Let love guide you through your day. Let it envelop you as
you close your eyes, breathe in the presence of God, and
turn your attention to him. May love be the choice you
make over and over again today. May it be the intention
you set in every interaction. Let it be what challenges you to
choose differently than you would going on autopilot.

Be purposeful in love. Be kind to those who cross your path
and include yourself in this. Offer yourself compassion,
just as you offer it to others. Choose peace over needing to
be right. Choose joy over having to make your point. Lean
into the love of God and let it fill you as often as you turn
your attention to the very near presence of God today!

A FRIEND IN DEED

*Offer grace to yourself and others
when you begin to get frustrated today.*

VESSELS OF GLORY

We now have this light shining in our hearts, but we ourselves are like fragile clay jars containing this great treasure. This makes it clear that our great power is from God, not from ourselves.

2 CORINTHIANS 4:7 NLT

The verse directly preceding this states that, "God is the one who has cascaded his light into us—the brilliant dawning light of the glorious knowledge of God as we gaze into the face of Jesus Christ" (TPT). The light of God shines in our hearts and we, though we are weak vessels in our humanity, reveal the glory of God at work within us.

May we look for the light of God's mercy shining through ordinary people as we go about our day. It doesn't matter how weak we may appear; God's love is strong. This is true for the person who is homeless, suffering with addiction, or experiencing an awful illness. May we not turn away from those who challenge our biases; let's turn toward them with compassion, knowing that God is as powerful for them as he is for us.

A FRIEND IN DEED

*Look beyond the outward appearances
of the people you meet today.*

HEIRS OF GOD

You are no longer a slave, but God's child;
and since you are his child,
God has made you also an heir.

GALATIANS 4:7 NIV

As heirs of the Father's kingdom with Christ, we have access to the endless resources through his Spirit. We are not beggars, and we are not slaves. Let us not shrink back in fear or play small because we think we don't deserve better. Let's be people who live large in faith, in love, and in the pursuit of peace.

The kingdom of God is constantly expanding. It grows like a tree that is planted by a river flourishes, blooms, and becomes a place of shelter for animals. Jesus likened the kingdom to a mustard seed: though it is the smallest of seeds, it grows into a large tree. It doesn't take more than a small seed of faith, so let's start with whatever we have no matter how small it may seem. God will tend to our small faith and grow it in the soil of his love.

A FRIEND IN DEED

Show a small gesture of love to a friend.

ROOM FOR HOPE

We are hard pressed on every side, but not crushed;
perplexed, but not in despair.

2 CORINTHIANS 4:8 NIV

When we go through troubling times, we may wonder why.
Instead of blaming ourselves, let's take our questions to
God. We don't have to pretend to understand why certain
things happen. We can trust his grace and mercy to guide
us. As long as we are breathing, there is room for hope.

The apostles went through suffering and persecution. So
did many, if not all, of the major characters in the Bible.
If they did, then why are we surprised when we do? Even
when we are confused, may we not give into despair. Let's
encourage our friends who may be going through a time
of bewilderment in their own lives, leaving room for their
process while also showing up in loving hope.

A FRIEND IN DEED

*Send flowers to a friend who is struggling
to make sense of their trial.*

ANYTHING WORTHY

Whatever is true, whatever is honorable, whatever is just, whatever is pure, whatever is pleasing, whatever is commendable, if there is any excellence and if there is anything worthy of praise, think about these things.

PHILIPPIANS 4:8 ESV

As you consider this verse today, read through it more than once. Whenever you find your mind wandering, turn it back to this verse. Is what you are thinking about true? Is what you are ruminating over honorable? Are the thoughts you are having toward the people in your life commendable? Don't let this lead you to a place of shame, but rather accept the challenge to move past your initial thoughts into a place of leadership over your thoughts.

When you think of your friends today, employ this same tactic. Is what you are thinking of them true? Is it honorable? Is it just? Is it pure? Is it worthy of praise? Turn your thoughts to what is honorable about your friends. What about their character is worthy of praise? Share it with them as an encouragement.

A FRIEND IN DEED

Share something that you respect about a friend today.

WHERE YOU ARE

Do not despise these small beginnings,
for the LORD rejoices to see the work begin.

ZECHARIAH 4:10 NLT

In friendship, it takes time to build trust. We cannot expect
to reap the benefits of an intimate relationship with people
we have just met. It takes hours together, getting to know
backgrounds and quirks. It takes vulnerability tested with
time. It takes showing up over and over again. It takes going
through hard times as well as good. It takes shared context
and a willingness to be real with each other.

Don't despair if you find yourself longing for deeper
relationships than you currently have. You cannot wish
yourself to the end point, but you can start where you
are and keep showing up and doing the work. The Lord
rejoices to see the work begin. He made us for relationship,
both with him and with others. Don't despise the small
beginnings, for there is infinite potential for growth.

A FRIEND IN DEED

*Ask someone you've been wanting to
get to know better out for coffee.*

EVERYTHING WITH INTENTION

Do you have the gift of speaking? Then speak as though God himself were speaking through you. Do you have the gift of helping others? Do it with all the strength and energy that God supplies. Then everything you do will bring glory to God through Jesus Christ. All glory and power to him forever and ever! Amen.

1 PETER 4:11 NLT

Whatever gifts you have, whatever strengths you bring to the table, be aware that God can use them for his glory. When you strategize, do it with integrity and for the common good. When you compose, do it as an offering of worship to the Lord. When you advise someone, do it with the Word as your reference and the character of God as your meter.

When we live with intention coupled with integrity, our lives reflect the glory of God. When we offer ourselves, our strengths, and our resources with love, we show that we are yielded to God's mercy, and he moves through us. We do not have to necessarily change what we do; perhaps we just need a perspective shift while we are doing it!

A FRIEND IN DEED

Use one of your strengths to help or bless a friend today.

CREATED BY GOD

You are worthy, our Lord and God, to receive glory and
honor and power, for you created all things, and by your
will they were created and have their being.

REVELATION 4:11 NIV

We were created by God's hand. Not only that, but we were
created to know him and to be known by him. We were made
to fit into a family with everyone working together. We are
each unique reflections of God's glory, and not one person
is exempt from this! Let's partner with God's heart and treat
others with the dignity and respect he has given them.

When we see people through the lens of God's loving hand
and heart, we can no longer excuse our prejudices. No
matter how different a person is from us, they are as worthy
of love, respect, kindness, care, and honor as we are. There
is beauty in the diversity of cultures in this world. May
we learn to embrace differences as opportunities to learn
something more about God.

A FRIEND IN DEED

*Instead of being threatened by differences,
let it be an opportunity to learn and embrace.*

THROUGH LOVE'S EYES

No one has ever seen God. But if we love each other, God
lives in us, and his love is brought to full expression in us.

1 JOHN 4:12 NLT

Though no one has ever seen God, we know the
characteristics of his nature. In verse sixteen of this same
chapter, John says, "God is love, and all who live in love live
in God, and God lives in them." *God is love.* Do we wonder
what God looks like? He looks like lovingkindness, mercy
that never ends, compassion that spreads from east to west,
and redemption.

The more we seek God, the more we spend time with him,
and the more we endeavor to be like him, the more we
will express his love. Perhaps we can ask a trusted friend
how we are doing in this department. What about us
communicates God's love? Which areas do we still need to
grow in? This is a vulnerable exercise and surely one to be
done with someone we trust and respect. But, oh, how we
can grow in love if we humbly lean into honest feedback!

A FRIEND IN DEED

*Ask a trusted friend if they would be willing
to do this exercise with you.*

A RESPECTABLE LIFE

People who are not believers will respect the way you live,
and you will not need to depend on others.

1 THESSALONIANS 4:12 NLT

There is a growing divide between what people of faith
deem to be their mission, especially in western culture, and
what the surrounding world thinks. If we get too caught up
in religious particulars, neglecting the call to self-sacrificial
love, then we are missing one of the main things that Christ
declared his followers do.

What do we get if we gain the favor of religious leaders, but
we neglect the poor and needy among us? May we seek to
lead lives that are full of integrity and honor, serving others
in compassion and being people of our word. Let's help
those who are in need, support those who are suffering, and
look to change our communities for the better. Instead of
looking for ways to make our lives more comfortable. Let
love move us in all things.

A FRIEND IN DEED

*Next time you spend time with a friend,
do something they enjoy.*

LIVING WORDS

The word of God is living and active and sharper than any two-edged sword, and piercing as far as the division of soul and spirit, of both joints and marrow, and able to judge the thoughts and intentions of the heart.

HEBREWS 4:12 NASB

Truth cuts deeply. It goes to our core, separating what we thought we knew from what we know to be true on a cellular level. The Spirit of God moves within us, making his truth ring deep within our souls. We don't have to search the world for revelation when the Spirit of God dwells inside us and brings the light of his wisdom to our lives. One word, one touch, one move, and we understand what we could not come to on our own.

We can trust God to help us, to lead us, and to instruct us. May we remain humble and teachable, no matter how old we grow or how much we have already learned in life. May we be open to receiving instruction from the Spirit no matter how it comes: through a friend, nature, or conversation. The Word of God is living and active, and it can appear anywhere at any moment, piercing our spirits and directing our hearts.

A FRIEND IN DEED

Offer words of encouragement to a friend.

EVEN IN SUFFERING

Rejoice inasmuch as you participate in the sufferings
of Christ, so that you may be overjoyed when his glory
is revealed.

1 PETER 4:13 NIV

Every trial is an opportunity to partner with Christ. Jesus
suffered, and yet he promises that when we suffer, we never
do it alone. God is our help and our strength. He is our
comfort and our support. Let us not give into the lie that
if we experience health crises, job loss, grief, or any other
suffering, that we are somehow outside of the will of God.
That does not line up with Scripture; it's just not true.

Every trial and trouble is a chance to know the fellowship of
God more deeply. The Spirit does not leave us when we are
in heartbreaking despair. He is close, he is full of hope and
love, and he does not let us go. May we find ways to look for
the light in dark days. May we choose to rejoice that God
is with us, even when we cannot see what he is doing. He is
faithful and trustworthy, and he won't fail.

A FRIEND IN DEED

Be a reason that someone rejoices today.

UNCOVERED

Nothing in all creation is hidden from God's sight.
Everything is uncovered and laid bare before the eyes
of him to whom we must give account.

HEBREWS 4:13 NIV

We cannot hide a thought or a motive from God. He sees
everything clearly. Though this may seem overwhelming,
it is good news for us. He cannot be fooled by lies or
be manipulated by the opinions of others. He knows us
through and through, and no one can coerce him out of his
love for us. What a reason to rejoice!

May we live with honor, knowing that God sees what
many try to hide. If there is something that we feel must
stay hidden within us, today is the day to lay it bare before
him and ask for his perspective. He sees it anyway. Is there
an area in which we are experiencing fear of being found
out? God breaks off clouds of shame as we are exposed in
his lifegiving light. May we be safe spaces for people of all
walks of life to confide in, just as Christ is.

A FRIEND IN DEED

Consider sharing a secret with someone you trust.

LIVING WATERS

"Anyone who drinks the water I give them will never be thirsty. In fact, the water I give them will become a spring of water in them. It will flow up into eternal life."

JOHN 4:14 NIRV

Jesus offers us salvation that does not expire. Once we drink the lifegiving waters of his mercy, we won't ever need to look anywhere else. We don't have to worry about a thing. And even when we do worry, God continues in faithfulness. May we approach our relationships with as much confidence as we have in Christ.

May we be people who love without measure, not putting stipulations on our loved ones to uphold in order for us to love them well. Love is something that we give, we practice, and we receive. We cannot control or manipulate others with love. If we were to try, it would end up being something other than love altogether. May we fill up on the living waters of God's presence within us, letting go of what we cannot control and trusting him to move in power and mercy.

A FRIEND IN DEED

Send a gift to a friend just because.

REACH OUT IN GRACE

All of this is for your benefit. And as God's grace reaches more and more people, there will be great thanksgiving, and God will receive more and more glory.

2 Corinthians 4:15 nlt

Isn't it wonderful how generous God is? He is always moving in mercy, expanding in grace, and overflowing in love. The resources of his kingdom never deplete. There is more than enough grace to reach every person. There is more than enough kindness to share. There is more than enough.

If we are running low on our own resources of grace and patience, we may need to take some time to recharge in the presence of God. He has an endless portion of grace. His grace empowers us to partner with his love in all things if we will choose it. May we first fill our own tanks with his love and then reach out in grace to those around us. There's always more to receive and there is much more that we can offer!

A FRIEND IN DEED

Be gracious to those you encounter today.

RELATABLE

He understands humanity, for as a Man, our magnificent
King-Priest was tempted in every way just as we are,
and conquered sin.

HEBREWS 4:15 TPT

Jesus truly understands the struggles we face. Not only
ideologically, like he *could* get why we would feel tempted.
He struggled with temptation as well. He was hungry,
irritable, tired, and weak. He experienced all the emotions
and trials that we face as humans. Even so, he overcame
every temptation and grew in grace and love.

We have the opportunity to lean into God's grace as he
relates to us. Just as he is gracious with us, let's choose to be
gracious with those around us. Is there a person in your life
you just can't understand? Do you struggle to understand
why they keep making the choices they do? Do their
struggles seem insurmountable? Jesus understands them as
much as he understands you.

A FRIEND IN DEED

*Pray for someone you struggle to understand,
knowing Christ gets it and he gets them!*

LIVE IN LOVE

We know how much God loves us, and we have put our
trust in his love. God is love, and all who live in love live
in God, and God lives in them.

1 JOHN 4:16 NLT

Does it seem like there is too much emphasis on love in
this devotional? If so, then know it is because the gospel
emphasizes the love of God over and over again! The love of
God is the most powerful force at work, for it is the nature
of God himself. There is more grace in his affection than we
could ever imagine. Instead of having concerns about going
too far in the name of love, let's consider that Christ gave
everything so that we might know that the Father loves us
more than we often allow ourselves to believe.

Stretch your imagination in love. It is not sacrilegious;
rather, it is the most holy thing you can do! No matter
what we do in this life, if we lack love, we miss the point.
Consider enlarging your capacity to love.

A FRIEND IN DEED

Don't put a limit on how loving you are today!

CARETAKER

Upon you I have leaned from before my birth;
you are he who took me from my mother's womb.
My praise is continually of you…
you are my strong refuge.

PSALM 76:6-7 ESV

God is our ultimate caregiver. He is both mother and
father: the source of our very being. And what a loving
and loyal caretaker he is! Psalm 139:13 says, "You formed
my inward parts; you knitted me together in my mother's
womb." Ephesians 2:10 says, "We are his workmanship,
created in Christ Jesus."

Not only were we created by God, but we are kept by him.
Psalm twenty-three says, "He leads me beside still waters.
He restores my soul." He leads us like the tender shepherd
and Father he is. Perhaps a friend needs to hear how
tenderly the Father cares for them today. No matter where
they are, God is present. He knows them and he loves them
completely!

A FRIEND IN DEED

*Encourage a friend by reminding them
of the Father's faithfulness.*

ETERNITY IN VIEW

We view our slight, short-lived troubles in the light of eternity. We see our difficulties as the substance that produces for us an eternal, weighty glory far beyond all comparison.

2 CORINTHIANS 4:17 TPT

Let us not lose sight of the hope of eternity in the glorious light of Christ's kingdom, no matter how dark our circumstances may seem at the moment. Though things may seem to get worse before they get better, daybreak is coming, and so is relief!

Let's persevere in faith, always choosing love and mercy, and promoting peace with our lifestyles. Even when we cannot see our way out of the trials in our lives, we are not alone. God is not stumped, and there is the loving connection and support of friends. May we never grow weary of doing good no matter the shortcuts that others take. Let's keep living in the light of God's love, for his love never fails.

A FRIEND IN DEED

Continue doing what God has shown you to do
and let the weight of others' expectations go.

MAY

Two are better than one,
Because they have a good
reward for their labor.

ECCLESIASTES 4:9 NKJV

FEAR-FREE LOVE

Such love has no fear, because perfect love expels all fear.
If we are afraid, it is for fear of punishment, and this shows
that we have not fully experienced his perfect love.

1 John 4:18 nlt

Perfect love is not motivated by fear. There is no looming
punishment or retribution lingering in God's heart as he
watches us. He is full of love that restores, liberates, and
redeems. May we partner always with his heart of pure
love and throw aside every form of care that seeks to
micromanage and control others.

When we are fully known and accepted as we are, we do
not worry that we will be found out. God is a loving Father,
and he welcomes us—weaknesses, warts, and all. May we
love others in this same way! May we let go of the need to
use fear as a motivator in our relationships. God's love does
not have conditions; does ours?

A FRIEND IN DEED

*Ask God to help you love others
without wanting to influence their choices.*

LOOK BEYOND

We don't look at the troubles we can see now;
rather, we fix our gaze on things that cannot be seen.
For the things we see now will soon be gone,
but the things we cannot see will last forever.

2 CORINTHIANS 4:18 NLT

When we are in a hard season, it can become all too easy to be dragged down by discouragement and hopelessness. As believers, we know that our present circumstances pale in comparison to the hope we have in Christ, so let's fix our attention on what is coming and what is ours now: the grace that is poured out upon us through fellowship with the Spirit.

Life is short; we know this all too well. Friends get sick and loved ones pass away. We experience financial problems, and it seems as though there is always a threat of war and conflict. May we look beyond the troubles we can see now and lean into the things that matter above all else.

A FRIEND IN DEED

Reach out and connect with a beloved friend today.

THE REASON

We love because he first loved us.

1 John 4:19 nrsv

When faced with reasons to withdraw love, grace, and mercy from those around us, let's look under the surface. We can prioritize health, safety, and peace through boundaries with those who take advantage of us while also extending grace. In fact, setting up boundaries with people like this can be one of the most loving acts we do.

In our relationships at large, even with those who are hard to deal with because of personality differences, we must remember that we don't simply choose to love others because we should but because we are recipients of endless love. Christ is our source in all things. We love because he first loved us. When we are running low on our own supply, let's turn to him and be filled with a fresh portion of his endless mercy! Then we will have more than enough to give while not running empty ourselves.

A FRIEND IN DEED

Cultivate compassion in your heart as you go about your day.

TESTIMONIES OF GOODNESS

This same God who takes care of me will supply all your
needs from his glorious riches, which have been
given to us in Christ Jesus.

PHILIPPIANS 4:19 NLT

It is good for our souls to remember how God has faithfully
provided for us in the past. If we have been met by tangible
acts of his mercy in our lives, then we have a story to tell.
Let's take some time to remember how God has come
through for us when we did not know what would happen.
Let's ask the Spirit to remind us of how good and how
present he has been.

Perhaps what comes to mind is a testimony of God's
faithfulness at work in someone else's life. That is not a
subpar response! Someone else's story can be a launching
pad for our own, boosting our faith and expectancy. God is
at work both in little and big ways, and if we ask him to give
us eyes to see where his mercy threads through our lives, he
will reveal where he has been working all along.

A FRIEND IN DEED

Share a testimony of God's provision
with a friend who needs to hear it.

POWERFUL KINGDOM

The kingdom of God does not consist in words
but in power.

1 CORINTHIANS 4:20 NASB

Debates are won through words, but the kingdom of God is not revealed in this way. It is not an argument to be won or an ideology to be put in places of political power. It is far greater than the systems of this world, and it is much more powerful than the agendas that humans tend to gravitate toward.

Let us look to the Lord, spend time in his presence, and ask him to reveal himself in our lives and in this world in power. The power of the Spirit can make the sick well, give peace to the tormented, encourage the hopeless heart, and even raise the dead back to life. There is nothing that the resurrection power of Christ cannot accomplish! He is able to do far more than we could ever dream, so let's let our faith rise with expectancy as we fellowship with him today.

A FRIEND IN DEED

Pray for God's power to be manifest in a friend's life.

RENEWED MINDSET

Let the Spirit renew
your thoughts and attitudes.

EPHESIANS 4:23 NLT

If we never challenge the thoughts and attitudes we were conditioned to believe, then we will never know the freedom and power of the renewal of our minds. How often do we allow shame to cover us as we wonder how a dark thought could have come into our minds? Or do we recognize that our minds take in more information than we could ever perceive and not every thought we have originates with us?

Instead of trying to dichotomize our thoughts into good and bad, perhaps we can get curious about them without instantly labeling. Why did we have such a strong reaction to that person's attitude? The Spirit renews our thoughts as we submit to him, and he delights in revealing the truth that lies under many of them. In Christ there is liberty, love, and grace. Let's apply that to our thought life as well.

A FRIEND IN DEED

When a friend shares a thought or opinion that does not align with what God says, challenge them in love.

SPIRIT AND TRUTH

"The time is coming—indeed it's here now—when true worshipers will worship the Father in spirit and in truth. The Father is looking for those who will worship him that way."

JOHN 4:23 NLT

What does it mean to worship the Lord in spirit and in truth? If that is what the Father is looking for, then we should understand what that looks like in our own lives. In this passage, Jesus was replying to a woman who was asking what physical place was the right place to worship God—Jerusalem or Mount Gerizim?

Jesus' response points to what he communicated time and time again through his ministry on the earth. True worshipers worship the Lord from a surrendered heart. It does not matter where we are, for the Spirit of God, given to us after Jesus ascended to heaven, is with us no matter where we go. We worship the Lord in the temple of our hearts, submitted to his truth and filled with his Spirit.

A FRIEND IN DEED

Share something you love about a friend with them.

THE WAY OF JESUS

Jesus was going throughout all Galilee, teaching in their synagogues and proclaiming the gospel of the kingdom, and healing every kind of disease and every kind of sickness among the people.

MATTHEW 4:23 NASB

Jesus did not just tell people about the love of God; he revealed it in tangible acts of mercy throughout his ministry. Wherever he went, he taught the people about the kingdom of God, what it is truly like, and then he performed miracles. He healed those who were sick, not only restoring their health but also their hope!

God has not stopped working in this way. If we venture to share the liberating gospel of God's grace with others, do we stop short after we share with words, or do we practically show the merciful kindness of God through our actions? Our words will fall flat if they are not backed up with how we live. May we be challenged to do a little more and say a little less today.

A FRIEND IN DEED

Offer to run an errand for a busy friend.

AN OPEN HEART

"For those who listen with open hearts will receive more revelation. But those who don't listen with open hearts will lose what little they think they have!"

MARK 4:25 TPT

Jesus says directly before this in verse twenty-four, "Be diligent to understand the meaning behind everything you hear, for as you do, more understanding will be given to you. And according to your longing to understand, much more will be added to you." When was the last time you spent time looking for the meaning behind what you heard whether it was in a conversation with a friend, a sensationalized news story, or an account of someone with a different lifestyle?

An open heart is not something to be wary about, for "those who listen with open hearts will receive more revelation." Curiosity should be something we celebrate, not something we fear. We often hear the trope "curiosity killed the cat," but looking to understand what we hear is how we gain knowledge. May we be people who put the tired tropes of fear aside and let our curiosity lead us into greater understanding.

A FRIEND IN DEED

Listen to a friend with an open heart.

A LIGHT LOAD

This is the love of God, that we keep his commandments.
And his commandments are not burdensome.

1 JOHN 5:3 ESV

When we truly love God, we follow his commands, not out of fear but out of reverence. God's grace is the empowering force that strengthens our love. His commands become a delight as we allow his mercy to permeate our hearts.

When we love someone, it is a delight to please them. We don't ignore their needs or desires. When we cook food for those we love and we see the joy on their faces, is it not a satisfaction to know that we aided in their delight? When a loved one expresses that they need something more from us, though it may sting at first, don't we endeavor to meet them in it? It is not ultimately burdensome to back our love up with our lifestyles. Let's live out our love in tangible acts of kindness.

A FRIEND IN DEED

Follow through on something you told a friend you would do.

HOLD ONTO HOPE

Hope does not put us to shame, because God's love has been poured into our hearts through the Holy Spirit who has been given to us.

ROMANS 5:5 ESV

It can feel silly to hold onto hope for something that seems far-off or unfeasible. But hope in God is never fruitless. What he has promised, he will do. What he has said will be fulfilled. Let's anchor our hope in his faithfulness, remembering his goodness. He never fails.

The Holy Spirit is as close as the skin on our bones. May we never forget the fellowship we have with the God of the universe here and now. All that we need is found in him. All that we long for is fulfilled by him. Let's hold onto hope and encourage our friends to do the same when they are wavering. God's love is a seal upon our hearts, and it is not just a nice idea; it is the power of God!

A FRIEND IN DEED

Encourage a friend by sharing your hopes for them with them.

WAITING FOR FULFILLMENT

"Blessed are those who hunger and thirst for righteousness, for they will be filled."

MATTHEW 5:6 NRSV

God promises that those who hunger and thirst for righteousness will be filled. These are Jesus' words. We find our satisfaction in him, and it's no passing feeling. Our soul's longings are and will be fulfilled in the bounty of Christ's love. When we crave goodness, longing to do what is right and for the justice of God to prevail, these cravings will not be left unsatisfied.

Do you have a friend who is active in serving others in love? Do you know someone who perseveres through hardship and gets into the trenches with those who are suffering? May their dedication to the love of God fuel you to go further in your own faith. Let the challenge of their lived-out love propel you in your own walk of submission to the Lord. Nothing is wasted when we do it unto God!

A FRIEND IN DEED

Thank a friend for their faithfulness
in both good times and hardship.

POUR IT ALL OUT

Pour out all your worries and stress upon him and leave them there, for he always tenderly cares for you.

1 PETER 5:7 TPT

We cannot escape the stresses of life, but we can give our worries to God. We cannot know what tomorrow will bring, but we can trust the one who does. We cannot be sure of our comfort, but we can be confident in the Comforter. When life has us spinning our wheels, let's pour out all our worries and stress upon the Lord, leaving them there, for he cares for us.

The worries and stresses of our lives are not only found in our singular selves but in our relationships, in the unknowns of diagnoses and other troubles. We can trust God with others as much as we trust him with ourselves. He is the same comfort, the same powerful God, the same redeemer for all of us. May we trust him with the worries of our friends as completely as we do for ourselves!

A FRIEND IN DEED

Step in to fill a need for a friend.

SETTLED IN CHRIST

May the God of all grace, who called us to His eternal glory
by Christ Jesus, after you have suffered a while, perfect,
establish, strengthen, and settle you.

1 PETER 5:10 NKJV

None of us are immune to suffering. In fact, in 1 Peter
5:9, Peter says, "the same sufferings are experienced by
your brotherhood in the world." Peter is speaking of the
suffering that comes from the activity of the devil. Not
every suffering is because some unseen force is attacking us,
but there are trials that we experience that we must resist
with faith.

As we persevere through suffering, the Lord will powerfully
restore us and make us stronger than we were. Who has
gone through a trial and does not know this to be true?
Though we wouldn't wish suffering on anyone, there is
a refining of character and faith that happens when we
endure.

A FRIEND IN DEED

*Text a friend an encouragement to keep enduring their trial
and remind them that it will not last forever.*

GREATER THAN FRIENDSHIP

If while we were still enemies, God fully reconciled us
to himself through the death of his Son, then something
greater than friendship is ours. Now that we are at peace
with God, and because we share in his resurrection life,
how much more we will be rescued from sin's dominion!

ROMANS 5:10 TPT

Friendship is a great gift. And yet, Christ has offered us
something more meaningful than friendship through his
salvation. We have peace with God and liberty in his love.
This means that he does not just relate to us with love, but
he has given us every benefit he has in order that we might
fellowship freely with the Father and dwell with him forever.

Think of your closest friend. Now imagine that you could
be around them all the time, no questions asked, no
distance between you. Imagine a relationship free from
conflict or assumption, just freedom to love and be loved.
No human relationship is perfect, but in Christ we find
fulfillment of every expectation and even more than that!
May we take hope in our communion with him, and may it
enrich every friendship we have.

A FRIEND IN DEED

Forgive a friend for an offense
that you have been holding onto.

KEEP BUILDING

Encourage one another and build one another up,
just as you are doing.

1 THESSALONIANS 5:11 ESV

What defines your relationships? What kinds of things do you spend time with your friends doing? Though you may not have hours-long deep conversations with every one of your friends, is there a depth and trust? Do you spend time encouraging each other, whether it's through a time of fun together or in reminding each other of what your strengths are?

Don't forget the importance of encouragement in your relationships. Though you don't have to gush over your friends every time you see them, be sure that you communicate what you enjoy about them. Be sure to affirm their hopes and be a trusted confidant. Everyone benefits from clear and helpful communication, so let's be up front about our encouragement and build each other up in love!

A FRIEND IN DEED

Tell a friend what impact they have had on your life.

HEARD

Here is what we can be sure of when we come to God in prayer. If we ask anything in keeping with what he wants, he hears us.

1 JOHN 5:14 NIRV

God hears our prayers. We know that when we come to him, we can be confident that he listens. Not only does he hear us, but he answers us. This is a key element of any relationship – to be heard and to receive. If we are only ever the ones sharing, then it may be one-sided. But in true friendship, even with the Lord, there is always give and take.

When was the last time you took the time to listen to a friend for more than a few minutes? Do you find yourself talking about your own problems more than you listen to theirs? Perhaps be more mindful of how well you are hearing those who reliably hear you. Let your need to share your own thoughts be weighed with how much room you are giving to theirs.

A FRIEND IN DEED

Initiate a conversation with a friend and spend more time listening than talking.

CONSIDER IT

And let us consider how we may spur one another on
toward love and good deeds, not giving up meeting
together, as some are in the habit of doing, but encouraging
one another—and all the more as you see the Day
approaching.

HEBREWS 10:24-25 NIV

With a crazy couple years behind us where we could
not gather with others as freely as we once could, have
you grown accustomed to spending less time with your
friends? Though there is nothing wrong with taking
safety precautions, we can still fellowship with others in a
meaningful way without putting ourselves or others at risk.

Maybe we found that when things got tough, our friendships
were more fragile and superficial than we once thought
them to be. Don't let that stop you from pursuing deep
relationships with others. We need each other, and you are
not alone in your longing for true friendship. Keep leaning
into love and looking for ways to show up and to meet with
those who will encourage you in your walk of faith.

A FRIEND IN DEED

Go on a walk with a friend.

COMPLETELY NEW

If anyone is in Christ, he is a new creation.
The old has passed away;
behold, the new has come.

2 Corinthians 5:17 esv

Our past does not dictate our future. When we are in Christ, he has removed the shame of our past and given us a new name. In the Old Testament, when someone had an encounter with the Lord, often they would be given a new identity. Sarai became Sarah. Abram became Abraham. In fact, this happened in the New Testament too. Saul became Paul.

Though we need not change our legal names, our identity in Christ makes us new people. He has reconciled us to himself, and we get to partner with him. Are there any grudges you've been holding against a loved one that you could let go of today? If it is in the past, can you let it go and make room for what is fresh, new, and true now?

A FRIEND IN DEED

Consider reaching out to someone who has expressed the desire to reunite and reconcile with you.

FREE OFFERINGS

I know, my God, that you search the heart, and take
pleasure in uprightness; in the uprightness of my heart I
have freely offered all these things , and now I have seen
your people, who are present here, offering freely and
joyously to you.

1 Chronicles 29:17 nrsv

Do you give love freely to those in your life, or do you stay
well-guarded? Consider those trusted friends and loved
ones who have shown that being vulnerable does not equal
being unsafe. Can you reach out a little more freely to them
today, sharing your heart with them?

Let your time and attention be a joyful gift you offer to
those you love. In a culture where we do not rest enough
and we always have more to accomplish, may you learn to
prioritize relationships over tasks that can be done at any
time. You will benefit from the time it takes to share a meal,
a walk, or a beverage with a friend. Make room for more
conversations and let your heart fill up on the offering of
love, both given and received.

A FRIEND IN DEED

Plan to meet a friend for a meal.

COUNT THE WAYS

In everything give thanks;
for this is God's will for you in Christ Jesus.

1 THESSALONIANS 5:18 NASB

How many things can you be grateful for today? In fact, how many things are you already thankful for? Take a few minutes before you move on with your day to list out all the things you can think of that you are grateful for right now. It can be as simple as the sunshine or a pet's cuddle or as profound as a job promotion or a good diagnosis.

As you turn your attention to what you are grateful for, may your heart grow in hope. Continue to look through eyes of thanksgiving as you move through your day. What can you be thankful for at work? What about in your family? Who are you grateful for and why? Let the eyes of your heart look with attentive detail at the many blessings you already have.

A FRIEND IN DEED

Share what you are grateful for with a friend.

MINISTRY OF RECONCILIATION

God has made all things new, and reconciled us to himself,
and given us the ministry of reconciling others to God.

2 CORINTHIANS 5:18 TPT

In reconciling us to himself, Jesus Christ has offered his
righteousness as our covering. He liberates us from the
requirements of the Law because he has fulfilled them. We
are brought into his kingdom of light and love, covered by
his blood. We are completely fresh and new in him! May we
be refreshed in his living love today, remembering that we
have been covered by his grace and mercy.

As we are filled with the confidence of his love, we get to
partner with his heart of reconciliation in sharing his mercy
with others. No one is exempt from the lengths of his love.
No one is kept outside of his gates of grace. He is full of
loyal love toward all, so let's join with him in extending
grace and mercy to everyone we encounter today!

A FRIEND IN DEED

*Don't wait for someone else to reach out to you today.
Pursue a friend!*

WORK OF LOVE

Make every effort to keep yourselves united in the Spirit,
binding yourselves together with peace.

EPHESIANS 4:3 NLT

Unity does not happen by accident, and trust is not built
haphazardly. Love is an active choice every single day. Are
we remaining open with the Spirit, spending time in prayer
and in the Word? Are we choosing to be gracious with our
loved ones and with those we struggle to get along with?

May we be known as people of peace, letting go of the need
to be on the same page about everything. There is far too
much to disagree about to get caught up in it. It does not
matter if we agree on everything, just that we choose to love
each other in spite of our faults! Let's show the grace that
we want to receive and keep our hearts open to one another
in love.

A FRIEND IN DEED

*Change the subject instead of getting in a debate
with a friend today. Choose peace!*

IMPORTANCE OF TODAY

God says, "At just the right time, I heard you.
On the day of salvation, I helped you."
Indeed, the "right time" is now.
Today is the day of salvation.

2 CORINTHIANS 6:2 NLT

When we are in the throes of the mundane, waiting for our breakthrough to come, we can forget the power of embracing the present. We don't have to be excited about every part of our lives in order to find glimmers of satisfaction within the ordinary. We don't have to abandon our dreams in order to find peace with what is accessible to us now.

Just as the Scripture says, "Today is the day of salvation," so is it the day that you have been given. The Spirit of God is fully accessible, and he is full of love, peace, joy, patience, kindness, and mercy toward you. Slow down a little and begin to notice the fruits of his presence in your life. Look for where his light shines through your friendships. Let today be the day you celebrate his gift of nearness.

A FRIEND IN DEED

Call a friend that you have been wanting to catch up with.

STEADFAST AS THE SUNRISE

"Let us acknowledge the LORD;
let us press on to acknowledge him.
As surely as the sun rises, he will appear;
he will come to us like the winter rains,
like the spring rains that water the earth."

HOSEA 6:3 NIV

God is the same yesterday, today, and forever. Today the sun will set behind the horizon and the stars will illuminate in the night sky. Tomorrow the sun will rise just as it has every day of your life. The rhythms of nature can remind us of the steadfast love of our Creator. He has not changed, and he has not forgotten what he said he will do.

How can you be intentional about acknowledging the Lord in your life and in your relationships today? He comes like the rains that water the earth. He shines like the sun, and plants and animals alike drink in the rays of his goodness. He brings life. May you find your heart buoyed in hope as you see the markers of his mercy in the world.

A FRIEND IN DEED

*Share a revelation you have had
of God's goodness with a friend.*

CULTIVATE CONTENTMENT

True godliness with contentment
is itself great wealth.

1 TIMOTHY 6:6 NLT

We do not need to have worldly wealth to know what
contentment is. Though money can certainly make
life easier, it is simply a resource. It is neither good nor
bad. When we become obsessed with making as much
as possible, hoarding our resources for our own self-
protection, we idolize what money can do for us. But the
truth is that contentment is found in peace with God, and
he has offered this to rich and poor alike.

How can you cultivate contentment with what you have?
What are you grateful for in your relationships? Take it a step
further and consider what you take for granted now that you
once longed for and wished for. What are those things? Can
you breed thankfulness in your heart as you trust God to
continue to care for you? May you find richer satisfaction in
the acknowledgment of God's faithfulness toward you than
in anything you could achieve on your own.

A FRIEND IN DEED

*Tell a friend what you are thankful for at present
and ask them to do the same.*

HE'S GOT IT

"Your Father knows exactly what you need
even before you ask him!"

MATTHEW 6:8 NLT

What are the worries that keep you up at night? What stresses have you found hard to shake? May this verse meet you precisely where you are and encourage your weary heart. It's already on his radar, beloved. He sees every area of your life that you are not even aware of yet. Will you turn to him for rest and peace?

Perhaps you are in a season of peace already, but you have a friend that is going through a great struggle. Instead of keeping your distance for fear of saying the wrong thing, show up in support of them. Have solidarity with them by bringing a meal, sending a note, or sharing this verse. Ask them what would be helpful and then implement it.

A FRIEND IN DEED

*Trust God with what you do not know
and share today's verse with a friend
who might need to hear it.*

HUMBLE KINDNESS

He has told you, O man, what is good, and what does the
LORD require of you. But to do justice, and to love kindness,
and to walk humbly with your God.

MICAH 6:8 ESV

The requirements of God's kingdom are not complicated.
The gospel is far simpler than we make it out to be. Why
would we try to add to God's great grace and mercy when
he has leveled the playing field for all? How do you practice
justice, show kindness, and walk humbly with your God?
These are the keys of living a life of laid-down love.

Consider your friends. Do you want what is best for them?
Do you get outraged when injustices are directed toward
them? Does kindness play a role in your relationship? Does
humility and openness play a part? More fiercely than
you love your friends is how God loves us. Let's reflect his
likeness in the simplicity of following his will and his ways.

A FRIEND IN DEED

*When you don't understand where a friend is coming from,
humble yourself and ask questions.*

EVEN IN HEARTACHE

Our hearts ache, but we always have joy.
We are poor, but we give spiritual riches to others.
We own nothing, and yet we have everything.

2 Corinthians 6:10 nlt

Paul learned how to find joy even in heartache. Many of
the followers of Christ have done the same. How can we
press into the delight of God and find joy, even in our own
heartbreak? We are never alone in our pain. The Holy Spirit
is our comforter and our peace. He is the most faithful
friend we could ever ask for.

Though no earthly friendship is perfect, we get tangible
glimpses of God's glory through true friends who show
up when the going gets tough. There is so much joy in
celebrating our successes with our friends, but there is also
joy to be found in the simple act of a friend offering us
their shoulder when we are burdened by the world. What a
wonderful glimpse into the faithfulness of God are true and
lasting friends!

A FRIEND IN DEED

Who has brought you joy in heartache?
Send them a small gift of gratitude today.

GRACIOUS FREEDOM

Sin is no longer your master, for you no longer live under
the requirements of the law. Instead, you live under the
freedom of God's grace.

ROMANS 6:14 NLT

Have you ever had a friend try to control your choices? Did
you think anything of it at the time? How did it make you
feel? True love is given and received freely. It is not dictated,
nor is it manipulated. We have received so much liberty in
the love of God, and that is the kind of liberty that we get
to offer our loved ones and friends as we love them with
hearts full of grace.

"Love is not jealous or boastful or proud or rude. It does
not demand its own way" (1 Corinthians 13:4-5). Do we
demand our own way in our relationships, or do we leave
room for differences in personality and choice? Let us
adopt the love of God as our ultimate model, letting go of
the need to control others. God is the best at leading us in
love, so let's trust him to do it!

A FRIEND IN DEED

Support a friend's individuality.

CHOSEN

"I will be a father to you,
and you shall be sons and daughters to Me."

2 CORINTHIANS 6:18 NASB

God has chosen us as his children. We are not part of some exclusive club. We are part of the family of his kingdom that is open to all who come to him! God is a gracious Father. He is patient and kind with us. He is gracious and understanding. May we be the same toward those we love.

We cannot choose what family we are born into, but we can choose those we share our lives with. There will be friends who are like family, communities where you have a place at the table, and a sense of belonging that is found in shared interests and mutual care. Let's keep choosing our circle of trusted friends, knowing we have agency in those we share our most vulnerable selves with. God is our gracious Father, and he has given us the opportunity to connect, cultivate, and love others as he loves us.

A FRIEND IN DEED

Thank God for your chosen family and friends today.

JUNE

Love prospers
when a fault is forgiven,
but dwelling on it
separates close friends.

PROVERBS 17:9 NLT

HE SEES IT ALL

"Your Father, whom you cannot see, will see you.
Your Father sees what is done in secret,
and he will reward you."

MATTHEW 6:18 NCV

We do not gain points with God by showing off our "righteousness." In this text, Jesus was addressing the issue of fasting. Instead of making themselves look miserable and disheveled, so that others would take notice, Jesus told his followers to maintain their cleanliness and not advertise their fasting.

Are there areas of our lives where we cannot stop complaining or making it obvious that we are doing all we can to maintain appearances of righteousness? We don't have to advertise our longings, our hopes, or our process with God to others. In fact, we know that God sees us. He sees what is done in secret, and he will reward us based on our hearts! He does not need loud prayers in order to answer them, and he does not need to be convinced.

A FRIEND IN DEED

*Resist giving unsolicited advice to a friend
when they share with you.*

RELIEF IS COMING

"God blesses you who are hungry now,
for you will be satisfied.
God blesses you who weep now,
for in due time you will laugh."

Luke 6:21 NLT

Though we may experience hunger now, our bellies will be filled. Those who weep will also find relief. When we hunger and thirst for righteousness, God promises to satisfy us. Though we grieve in this life, we will feel the delight of joy again. Psalm 30:5 says it this way: "Weeping may last through the night, but joy comes in the morning."

Can you think of a friend who is experiencing sorrow? Have they begun to lose hope that they will ever find relief? May you encourage them with comfort and be a safe place to dare them to dream of better days. There is an end to every dark night. Just as the sun rises each morning, so will times of laughter and rejoicing come again.

A FRIEND IN DEED

Bring lightheartedness into your friendships:
watch a funny movie, tell jokes, share comical experiences!

TRUST HIM

"Look at all the birds—do you think they worry about
their existence? They don't plant or reap or store up food,
yet your heavenly Father provides them each with food.
Aren't you much more valuable to your Father than they?"

MATTHEW 6:26 TPT

Have you ever watched animals get ready for the different
seasons? Like clockwork, they begin to store nuts and build
warm nests in the autumn. Many birds migrate to warmer
climates. They don't worry about their existence. They
simply live it. They have intuition built within them, and so
do we.

Can we let go of the need to dictate how mild or harsh the
seasons will be and just prepare ourselves and trust that
God will take care of us? There is relief on a hot day in the
shade. There is warmth by a fire in the winter cold. Let's
give up the worry of what we cannot begin to predict or
control and instead give our attention to what is ours to do.
God will take care of the rest.

A FRIEND IN DEED

*Whenever you start to worry, say a prayer of thanks
and release it.*

CALL TO REST

"Come away by yourselves to a secluded place and rest a while." (For there were many people coming and going, and they did not even have time to eat.)

MARK 6:31 NASB

The way of Christ does not dictate that we push ourselves to our breaking points. There will be time to sacrifice and time to refuel and care for ourselves. Rest is not just important to our lives; it is necessary. Jesus invited his disciples to escape the crowds and go off to a secluded place to rest and rejuvenate. It is okay and even *holy* for us to do the same!

When was the last time you went away with a friend? When was the last time you made space in your schedule to even spend an afternoon or evening with one, relaxing and doing what is lifegiving for you both? May you recognize the power of prioritizing rest, not only in your life, but also restful practices in your relationships.

A FRIEND IN DEED

Plan uninterrupted time with a friend doing something restful for both of you.

A RIGHTEOUS CHOICE

"Overflow mercy and compassion for others,
just as your heavenly Father overflows with mercy
and compassion for all."

LUKE 6:36 TPT

Directly before this verse, Jesus says, "Be like your Father who is famous for his kindness to heal even the thankless and cruel." We show our Christlikeness when we refuse to withhold mercy and compassion from others no matter what they have done. This is not the same as allowing them access to our lives. We can be merciful and compassionate and still set up boundaries with people we don't trust.

When we choose compassion over judgment and mercy over hatred, we align our lives with the love of God. When we choose to be kind to those who refuse to give us the same courtesy, we offer love without the need for anything in return. How we choose to act and interact should not be based on what we can receive from others. It should come from a deep place of confident acceptance in the love of Christ that overcomes all.

A FRIEND IN DEED

Give a gift without expecting anything in return.

COME TO HIM

"All that the Father gives me will come to me,
and whoever comes to me I will never cast out."

JOHN 6:37 ESV

Jesus promises that when we come to him, we will be embraced by him and never turned away. In verse thirty-nine he goes on to say, "This is the will of him who sent me, that I should lose nothing of all that he has given me, but raise it up on the last day." He isn't speaking of things, but of the people who come to him.

The longing of the Father is that all who embrace Jesus and believe in him will experience eternal life in his kingdom. He is not waiting for us to fail or looking for a reason to kick us out. That is not how his love works! He is endlessly merciful and faithful to do what he has promised. We don't have to fear for our future when we trust in Jesus.

A FRIEND IN DEED

Encourage a friend to turn to Jesus in wholehearted trust no matter what they are going through.

JUDGMENTAL ATTITUDES

Jesus said, "Forsake the habit of criticizing and judging others, and then you will not be criticized and judged in return. Don't look at others and pronounce them guilty, and you will not experience guilty accusations yourself. Forgive over and over and you will be forgiven over and over."

LUKE 6:37 TPT

Have you ever noticed that church culture can sometimes breed criticism and judgment? This is not the way of Christ. He clearly commands us to throw away the habit of picking another person apart, offering kindness and grace instead. When we speak of the love of Christ in our lives, yet harbor bitterness toward others, we are being hypocritical. Let's be sure that we are living with integrity and not with double standards.

We don't have the right to look at others' lives and "pronounce them guilty," as Jesus said. There is a place for accountability and justice when people are being abused. This is not what Jesus is speaking of here. What are our habits with others? Are they to build each other up or to look for ways to tear others down? Let's keep practicing forgiveness and mercy, for the Father is forgiving toward us.

A FRIEND IN DEED

Refrain from gossiping about people today.

FILLED WITH COMFORT

I am filled with comfort.
In all our affliction,
I am overflowing with joy.

2 CORINTHIANS 7:4 ESV

Do you have a close friend that is a comforting presence in your life? Who do you turn to when things go sour? Who do you reach out to when life gets hard? Hopefully, you are connected in all the ups in life and not just the downs. But a friend who can be a comfort in our darkest times is a gift from God indeed.

Instead of marveling at those people in our lives who seem to never skip a beat or get down about their situations, let's learn to ask them how they got to where they are. Let's lean into the backstory and let them share their stories of God's nearness, his faithfulness, and his comfort. We don't have to force a smile through our pain, but God will give us joy when we look to him.

A FRIEND IN DEED

*Ask a respected friend how God
has shown his love to them in times of hardship.*

FAITHFUL ONE

"Know therefore that the LORD your God is God;
he is the faithful God, keeping his covenant of love
to a thousand generations of those who love him
and keep his commandments."

DEUTERONOMY 7:9 NIV

When we choose to love God with our hearts, souls, minds, and strength, he honors our submission. We cannot know to what lengths his love goes. We cannot see the threads of his mercy that are sewn through our lives into the world around us. All there is, when everything else is said and done, is love. That is the greatest of the things that Scripture says will remain.

We do not earn the mercy of God; we receive it. We act on it. We are filled by it and practice giving it away to others. We live it. God is faithful, regardless of our actions, to that which he has declared. But why would we not partner with him when he is endlessly good, and he works all things together for the good of those who love him?

A FRIEND IN DEED

Share a testimony of God's faithfulness with a friend today.

OVERFLOWING COMPASSION

> When the Lord saw her,
> his heart overflowed with compassion.
> "Don't cry!" he said.
>
> LUKE 7:13 NLT

Jesus allowed himself to be completely overcome by a mother's grief in this text. He identified with her depth of sorrow. This is the deepest level of compassion that overflowed from his heart. He did not simply see or acknowledge her pain, but he felt it for himself. Have you ever experienced this? Have you ever felt compassion sweep over you so fully that another's sorrow became your own?

Compassion sounds like a nice and simple concept, and yet it can move our hearts so mightily that we feel what another feels. We often speak of empathy in this way. Jesus, overcome by a mother's sorrow over losing her child, urged her not to cry, not because he was insensitive, but because he was about to fix her problem. He raised her son from the dead that day. How can we let compassion move our hearts into action?

A FRIEND IN DEED

Let your heart be moved with the compassion of Christ today and follow through on an urge you have to help.

CONTINUE ON YOUR PATH

Each one of you should continue to live the way God has given you to live—the way you were when God called you.

1 CORINTHIANS 7:17 NCV

Have you felt the pressure to become someone you don't recognize? Do you believe that in order to make a difference for the kingdom of God, you have to give your time and energy to full-time ministry? The Lord has equipped you as you are. He can use every gifting, talent, and skill that you already have, for his glory. Do you want to build a better business? Do all things with integrity. Do you want to continue in sales? Do it for God's glory.

Whatever you are skilled at is an opportunity to reflect God's mercy and character through it. What of your friends? Who do they know you to be? What are the strengths they already see in you? Unless God makes a way for you to walk a new path, put your hand to what is already yours. He can and will use it all for his glory!

A FRIEND IN DEED

Encourage a friend by sharing what strengths you see in them.

EVERYTHING MADE RIGHT

I will give all my thanks to you, Lord,
for you make everything right in the end.
I will sing my highest praise
to the God of the Highest Place!

PSALM 7:17 TPT

No matter where we are in our journey, whether it's in the messy middle of a transition or in the beginning of a new venture, God will make everything right in the end. Even when we think we are at our end, if it isn't right or good, it's not the end of what God is doing. We cannot escape trouble or trials. We already know this to be true. And we cannot control how our lives will end. But even when our bodies fail us, God is not done working. We will know incomparable joy, peace, love, and satisfaction in the fullness of his kingdom in eternity.

What can you give thanks for in your life today? What areas of trouble can you be grateful for? It may take some digging beyond the surface to recognize where the light meets us in our suffering. Every day is an opportunity to take hold of God's great grace. There is more at work than what we see, and God will continue to make everything right in his time.

A FRIEND IN DEED

Finish a project you have been meaning to pass along to a friend.

FREE FROM BLAME

There is therefore now no condemnation
for those who are in Christ Jesus.

ROMANS 8:1 ESV

The book of Romans illustrates our freedom in Christ. When
we come to the Lord offering our hearts and our faith, we
are covered by the mercy of God that purifies us. He is our
righteousness, and we don't have to worry about striving for
perfection. He has declared us pure in his sight, and no one
can take that away. There is not now "some condemnation"
for those who are in Christ Jesus; there is none!

Do you know a friend who is struggling with their self-
worth? Can they not move past the narrative of shame or
guilt that says if they just do more, want less, etc., then
they will be ready to receive the liberating love of God in
full? Pray for them to receive revelation of their freedom
in Christ, right here and now. God will never blame us
for what he has already forgiven. Psalm 103:12 states, "as
far as the east is from the west, so far does he remove our
transgressions from us."

A FRIEND IN DEED

*Share God's unconditional love with a friend
who needs to be reminded today.*

NOTHING IS IMPOSSIBLE

This is what the LORD of Heaven's Armies says:
"All this may seem impossible to you now, a small remnant
of God's people. But is it impossible for me?"
says the LORD of Heaven's Armies.

ZECHARIAH 8:6 NLT

With God, all things are possible. When he speaks, do we take him at his word, or do we look at the impracticality of his promises and think it's just not possible? Though with our limited resources it may seem improbable for us, *nothing* is impossible for the Lord God, Creator of the universe.

Sometimes we need to be reminded that human logic can only take us so far. There are mysterious and mystical forces at work in the Spirit of God. What God declares he will do will be done. He is faithful to his Word. He is faithful to his promises. We don't need to see how it will all work out in order to put our faith in him. His nature is tried and true, and he won't fail us now. He never changes.

A FRIEND IN DEED

Share today's verse with a friend who is waiting on a promise.

BUILD UP GENEROSITY

You are rich in everything—in faith, in speaking,
in knowledge, in truly wanting to help,
and in the love you learned from us. In the same way,
be strong also in the grace of giving.

2 Corinthians 8:7 ncv

The kingdom of God is not only found in spiritual practices, but in very practical ones as well. If we claim to love God and to follow him with our lives, then our lifestyles and choices will reflect it—down to how we interact with strangers.

God is incredibly generous. He gives without asking for anything in return. He never stops offering more of his mercy, kindness, grace, and wisdom. There is always more to discover in him. He is greater than we could ever imagine! As his children, do we reflect his generosity with our own? Do we give to others without needing it to be returned? Do we determine to share what we have, or do we hoard what we have earned? May we be people of great generosity, growing strong in the grace of giving for our Father's storehouses are endless, and he will provide for us.

A FRIEND IN DEED

Give a generous gift to someone today.

UNQUENCHABLE LOVE

Many waters cannot quench love;
rivers cannot sweep it away.
If one were to give all the wealth of one's house for love,
it would be utterly scorned.

SONG OF SOLOMON 8:7 NIV

The love of God is far from limited. There is a river in the hills of Bosnia where the waters come rushing out from the side of a mountain. It doesn't trickle; it flows wide, fast, and pure, directly from the source underneath. It is a startling picture of God's unquenchable love that comes rushing straight from his heart without delay.

May we go straight to the source of love today. There, may we experience the lifegiving purity of his affection that never ebbs. May we be rocks in the river of our God, firmly established in his love, letting it wash over us and move us to where he wants us to go. There is nothing greater than experiencing the lifegiving empowerment of God's powerful mercy!

A FRIEND IN DEED

Fill up on God's love and then share it those you meet today.

WALK IN THE LIGHT

"I am the Light of the world; he who follows Me will not walk in the darkness, but will have the Light of life."

JOHN 8:12 NASB

When we follow Jesus, we walk in the light of his truth. When we apply his living words and teachings to our lives, we can be sure that we are on the path of his righteousness. We cannot simply say that we love Jesus, never apply his wisdom to our lives, and expect transformation. If we truly love someone, we will take what they say to heart and implement it in our lives.

How does the light of God lead you on a day-to-day basis? How does it affect and inform your relationships? Make it simple today and read through Jesus' words in the gospels. Where do you feel a challenge? Where do you feel relief? Let his words guide you in practical ways.

A FRIEND IN DEED

Spend time with Jesus today and ask him to show you ways to bless a friend with the light of his truth.

REMEMBER THIS

"Nothing is hidden that will not be made manifest, nor is anything secret that will not be known and come to light."

LUKE 8:17 ESV

It can be discouraging when we are living the best we know how, with integrity, honor, honesty, and justice, yet it seems as though those with ulterior motives and those looking for shortcuts that benefit only themselves, are successful. Instead of becoming overly critical and disheartened, let's remember that God sees everything. Nothing will remain hidden forever. Those who are cheating their way through life will be held accountable.

Can we be people who continue to walk in the light of God's merciful kindness? Can we continue to choose generosity? Can we do what we know to do because God has transformed our lives in his love? Let's look to him when we cannot stand to look at the world around us any longer. There is hope, healing, and a future in him.

A FRIEND IN DEED

Encourage a friend to keep persevering in love
even when they are discouraged.

INTERCESSION

The Spirit also helps our weakness; for we do not know how
to pray as we should, but the Spirit Himself intercedes for
us with groanings too deep for words.

ROMANS 8:26 NASB

When we don't know how to pray, the Spirit of God himself
steps in to intercede for us. We don't have to have the right
words, know the right outcome, or even use words at all
in order to lift up our hearts in prayer. The Spirit of God
translates our feelings into prayers that are lifted before the
throne of the Father.

Jesus spent time interceding, and so should we. Prayer is
not just for the settling of our hearts, but also for our hearts
to align with God's purposes for the world and the people
around us. When was the last time you interceded for a
friend? When did you spend time turning your thoughts
about their circumstances into prayers? Even if you don't
know what to pray, let your heart allow the Spirit to
intercede on their behalf.

A FRIEND IN DEED

Spend time in intercession for a friend.

UNCONTAINABLE

> "Will God indeed dwell on the earth?
> Behold, heaven and the highest heaven cannot contain You,
> how much less this house which I have built!"
>
> 1 KINGS 8:27 NASB

Jesus will one day return and make all wrong things right.
Though the highest heavens cannot contain him, he will
invite us into the physical kingdom of his reign. Just as the
wind cannot be contained, neither can the Spirit of God.
We cannot imagine how great the Lord is and how vast
his love. He comes close and reveals himself to us through
fellowship with his Spirit.

No one person, no one church, no one community, no one
nation, and not even this earth can contain the complexity
of God. He is vaster than we can account for. Let's allow the
Lord to broaden our understanding of him through various
and diverse expressions in the earth. We do not know all
there is to know, and we have not tasted the fullness of his
glory!

A FRIEND IN DEED

*Look for ways to learn about God through friends
who are different than you are.*

THREADS OF MERCY

We are convinced that every detail of our lives is continually woven together to fit into God's perfect plan of bringing good into our lives, for we are his lovers who have been called to fulfill his designed purpose.

ROMANS 8:28 TPT

God is able to weave even what seems irredeemable to us into the tapestry of his merciful plan and purpose. He includes the details that most would overlook, and he threads his glorious redemption through our lives. He is just that good! In fact, he is far better than we can imagine.

When you look at your friends' lives, where do you see God's mercy weaved? Perhaps communicate to them today where you see his hand and restorative power at work. What is so clear to you, they may not even notice. Look for where God has brought good into their lives and remark on it. They may just return the favor.

A FRIEND IN DEED

As you pray for a friend, ask the Holy Spirit to highlight where he is working in their life.

ALIGNED WITH CHRIST

What should we say then?
Since God is on our side,
who can be against us?

ROMANS 8:31 NCV

How can God's love be proven? It is through Jesus that the true heart of our merciful Father is revealed. It is through fellowship with the Spirit that we experience the lifegiving and transformative power of his mercy. We don't need to fear the unknowns of tomorrow or how things will play out. God is with us, and he will not leave us. He is our perfect peace, our steady source, and our help in times of trouble.

Do you see an area where a friend seems to be standing alone? Do you know that God's mercy is for them? Where they are longing for justice, you can show up. Stand with them in solidarity and let your supportive presence encourage their hearts in God's help. You can be a tangible instrument of God's faithful love to someone today.

A FRIEND IN DEED

Look for a way to stand in solidarity with a friend.

PROVEN AND TESTED

God has proved his love by giving us his greatest treasure,
the gift of his Son. And since God freely offered him up as
the sacrifice for us all, he certainly won't withhold from us
anything else he has to give.

ROMANS 8:32 TPT

The Gospel centers around Christ. It all revolves around
the good news of his coming, the revelation he brought of
the Father, and the sacrifice of his life to make a way for
us to have full and lasting fellowship with God. He was
resurrected and is alive. The power of sin, death, and shame
were broken under his grave-busting mercy.

There is more than knowledge in Christ. There is more than
faith to acquire. There is love, joy, peace, patience, kindness,
and so much more. All the fruits of God's Spirit reveal the
nature of his kingdom. They are tangible markers of his
goodness and his reign. Where there is darkness now, there
will be light. Where there is opposition now, there will
be freedom. Where there is resistance now, there will be
breakthrough. Let's press into the proven love of God and
be liberated in his grace today!

A FRIEND IN DEED

*Offer your time to a friend through a phone call,
a coffee date, or a walk.*

UNEQUIVOCALLY FREE

"If the Son sets you free,
you are truly free."

JOHN 8:36 NLT

Jesus puts no conditions on the liberty of his love. We are free—truly free! We live in the light of his merciful kindness and walk without shame in our lives. Though there can be many caveats in contracts, the grace of God gives freedom without demerit and with no hidden requirements. If you have been set free by the Son of God, then you are truly free. Leave that shame and blame behind and walk confidently in his love and light.

Don't we want our loved ones to walk in confidence and freedom? Don't we want the best for them in all things? Though we may not agree with all their choices, it is not our job to micromanage their lives. God is able to direct those who look to him. Trust your friends to his great grace. He's got it, and he's got them.

A FRIEND IN DEED

*Give a friend the freedom to choose
what you will do together next.*

TELL A FRIEND

"Return to your home, and declare how much God has
done for you." So he went away, proclaiming throughout
the city how much Jesus had done for him.

LUKE 8:39 NRSV

When God moves on our behalf, do we just keep going on
with our lives, or do we go back to our home, family, and
friends and share it with them? Let's not just move on with
business as normal when the mercy of God moves. Let's
take time to tell others, especially those who know us well.
Our blessing can become a shared blessing.

Think of the last time you heard really good news from a
close friend. Did you not celebrate as if it had happened
to you? Did you not feel joy deep within your heart? Let
your victories be shared! Miracles of God's mercy are
meant to be an encouragement, not only to those of us who
experience them, but also to those with whom we share life.

A FRIEND IN DEED

Share with a dear friend what God has revealed to you.

PRINCE OF PEACE

"A child has been born to us; God has given a son to us.
He will be responsible for leading the people.
His name will be Wonderful Counselor, Powerful God,
Father Who Lives Forever, Prince of Peace."

ISAIAH 9:6 NCV

Jesus came to reveal the heart of the Father, but he also came as the promised Messiah and Savior for a world caught in the cycle of sin and death. He broke the cycle, removed the yoke of slavery, and offered us a way into full fellowship with the mercy of God. He is our leader, and this is as true today as it was when he ministered on the earth. He is as reliable in love now and as worthy of our trust as he ever was or will be.

Jesus is our Prince of Peace. Do you know someone who is struggling to find and maintain peace in their lives? Does fear and anxiety keep them from living freely? There is no judgment or blame. The world is full of reasons to worry. May we be people of peace. May we offer ourselves as comforters and joy-bringers. May we be tenacious and persistent, loving and pursuing peace with each other.

A FRIEND IN DEED

*Be a person of peace to someone
who is struggling with fear today.*

INCOMPARABLE WISDOM

How happy your people must be! How happy your officials,
who continually stand before you and hear your wisdom!

2 CHRONICLES 9:7 NIV

Wisdom is a tremendous gift. The Book of Proverbs
illustrates the treasures of God's wisdom in various ways.
Proverbs 8:11 says, "Wisdom is more precious than rubies,
and nothing you desire can compare with her." Wisdom is
more than knowledge. It is shrewd and smart, but it is also
full of discretion and discernment.

What kind of advice do we offer our friends when they seek
it? Do we pass on what we have observed or have heard
to be true? Do we offer our lived experience, knowing
there is room for other points of view? First and foremost,
let's continue to seek the wisdom of God as if it's all that
matters. The wisdom of God is better than treasure!

A FRIEND IN DEED

Avoid giving black and white answers
where there is obvious ambiguity. Be ready
to admit when you don't know something.

INTENTIONAL GIVING

Each of you should give what you have decided in your
heart to give. You shouldn't give if you don't want to.
You shouldn't give because you are forced to.
God loves a cheerful giver.

2 CORINTHIANS 9:7 NIRV

How often do we use guilt as a motivator in our
relationships? Hopefully, it is rare, but there is always grace
to change. Let's be really honest with ourselves: are we
clear about what we do or don't want to give? Do we allow
others the chance to opt out of things? Do we let ourselves
be guilted into giving what we would never give on our
own simply because we wanted to live up to someone else's
expectation?

There is a difference between challenging someone and
guilting them. God loves a cheerful giver. How intentional
are we with generosity? Do we make it clear with our loved
ones that they can be as intentional as they want without
judgment of what it looks like to us? Let's take ownership of
our own choices and allow others to do the same without
guilt.

A FRIEND IN DEED

*Decide in your heart how you want to bless a friend
and go out of your way to make it happen this week.*

SUPPLIER

God supplies seed for the person who plants. He supplies
bread for food. God will also supply and increase the
amount of your seed. He will increase the results
of your good works.

2 Corinthians 9:10 nirv

Though we may work hard for what we have, we must
realize that it is all temporary. We cannot take anything
with us when we leave this life. Have we set our hopes
in what we can accomplish here, what we can buy or
how much land we can own? Or do we let the focus and
attention of our heart be on the relationships we cultivate?
Our memory can live on in our loved ones, but the stuff
that we accumulate will move on without us.

Give thanks to God for what you have today. Let your heart
be grateful for what God has supplied you with to live:
the bread to fill your belly, the shelter to house you, the
relationships to make you feel seen, known, and loved. May
we keep our focus on how we can build a lasting legacy
through relationships.

A FRIEND IN DEED

Buy a potted plant for a friend.

PROMISES OF RESTORATION

Return to the stronghold, you prisoners of hope.
Even today I declare that I will restore double to you.

ZECHARIAH 9:12 NKJV

The God of restoration and redemption does not simply return our losses; he gives us a double portion. Has a hard season of the soul ravaged your life? Did you lose what felt like too much? Take hope in the Lord today and let this verse be a beacon of promise to you. Your God will restore what was taken, and he will multiply it.

Who can you share this message of hope with today? Is there a friend who has also struggled to hold onto the expectation of God's coming goodness? May you take their hand and pray Psalm 27:13 over them: "I would have lost heart, unless I had believed that I would see the goodness of the Lord in the land of the living." You will see the goodness of the Lord again!

A FRIEND IN DEED

*Send a friend an encouraging song
that makes you think of them.*

JULY

A man of many companions
may come to ruin,
but there is a friend
who sticks closer than a brother.

PROVERBS 18:24 ESV

STUDY MERCY

"You should go and study the meaning of the verse: I want you to show mercy, not just offer me a sacrifice. For I have come to invite the outcasts of society and sinners, not those who think they are already on the right path."

MATTHEW 9:13 TPT

When was the last time you truly considered what Jesus said here? What do you think it looks like for you to show mercy in your lifestyle and not just offer God sacrifice? How do you think this applies to how you choose to interact with others, both friends and strangers alike?

Jesus was clear in his teachings that he was not sent to heal those who are well. He wasn't there to love certain people and cast others aside. He reached out to the outcasts often, breaking the religious expectations of the day. Do we go out of our way to extend kindness to those others avoid? Do we choose to live with love as our main motivation? May we take Jesus' words more seriously than even the words of those we respect most, knowing that his lead is always the one to follow.

A FRIEND IN DEED

Think about how you can show mercy
in tangible ways to your friends.

MERCIFUL ONE

It depends not on human will or exertion,
but on God, who has mercy.

ROMANS 9:16 ESV

God's mercy is unequivocally dependent on him and not on us. God's kindness is freely offered. It is not given in greater measure to those who try to earn it. It is overwhelmingly abundant, and it is God's choice to give to all whom he chooses.

Have you fallen into the habit of trying to earn God's favor or affection? Have you tried to prove to him, yourself, or others that you are worthy of his love? In truth, it is a wasted effort to strive, for you have his mercy whether or not you crave it. Does this mean you should give up altogether? By no means. May you live from a place of secure love rather than trying to earn what is already freely yours. When you are free in his mercy, you can choose how you will live from a place of grounded and humble love.

A FRIEND IN DEED

*Instead of trying to earn your friends' affections,
simply be yourself and show up as you are.*

HELP TO BELIEVE

Immediately the boy's father exclaimed, "I do believe; help me overcome my unbelief!"

MARK 9:24 NIV

Life is not a clear, dichotomous path. There are many paths that lie between the extremes we so often paint as our true reality. God can deal with ambiguity, but can we? It is possible to hold two seemingly opposing feelings at the same time. We can believe the Lord and also recognize that there are parts of us that don't know how to believe.

God is our help in all things, even in our feeble faith! We don't have to pretend to have it all together and figured out, for he knows us inside and out already. He sees the areas of quiet confidence and also the parts of us that struggle with doubt. He does not condemn us for our questions. He meets us in them, and he strengthens us with his Spirit. May we also allow for the complexity of feelings within our friends and loved ones. There is room for more than one feeling or perception at a time.

A FRIEND IN DEED

Share an area with a friend where you have mixed feelings.

BENEFITS OF TRAINING

Everyone who competes in the games goes into strict
training. They do it to get a crown that will not last,
but we do it to get a crown that will last forever.

1 CORINTHIANS 9:25 NIV

Lifestyles do not happen by accident. Do we have goals
that we want to reach but are not getting very far? We must
break down day-to-day how we will work toward those
goals in order to make movement. Athletes do not simply
show up at their events and play, hoping for the best. They
go into strict training in order to perform at their best.

We must do the same if we want to experience growth in
any area, including in our relationships. If we want to be
closer to our friends, we need to schedule times and be
intentional about connecting! We need to make plans and
put them on our calendars and then follow through. Every
area of life benefits from intention and application. What
can you do today to implement more intentional practices
to deepen your friendships?

A FRIEND IN DEED

*Plan a time to get together with a friend in the next
couple of weeks and make it recurring if you can.*

GRACIOUS GOD

In Your great mercy You did not
utterly consume them nor forsake them;
For You are God, gracious and merciful.

NEHEMIAH 9:31 NKJV

God is generously gracious toward us. He has not reached
the limits of his loving patience. What a wonderfully good
Father he is! May we spend time today meditating on his
goodness, his kindness, and his faithfulness toward us.

When was the last time you flew off the handle when you
lost patience with a loved one? What a common human
experience this is! It's not really a question of if it will
happen, but when. How we repair our relationships after an
incident like this is where we can put grace into practice,
both with ourselves and with our loved ones. God who is
gracious strengthens us as we humbly reconcile with those
we have hurt. Let's not simply move on from a break like
this, but let's take the time to communicate and lovingly
repair the damage with our people.

A FRIEND IN DEED

*Have a respectful conversation with a friend
with the intention of resolving a past hurt.*

ABILITY TO CHOOSE

"No one takes it from me,
but I lay it down of my own accord.
I have authority to lay it down,
and I have authority to take it up again.
This charge I have received from my Father."

JOHN 10:8 ESV

We often speak about Jesus as a lamb being led to the slaughter at the end of his life. The truth is that he knew what was coming and he willingly chose to submit to it. Do we give the power of our personal choice away when hard circumstances hit? Do we feel powerless in the face of other people's expectations or decisions?

We certainly cannot choose everything that happens in our lives, but we can choose how we will react. Will we harbor bitterness, or will we leave room for mercy to grow? Do we recognize where we still have personal choice in how we will move forward in healing, even after we were hurt by someone? We cannot control anyone else, but we can choose how we will grow from where we are planted.

A FRIEND IN DEED

Take ownership of your choices in your relationships.

FEARLESS CONFIDENCE

The one who walks in integrity
will experience a fearless confidence in life,
but the one who is devious will eventually be exposed.

PROVERBS 10:9 TPT

Why would someone who walks in integrity experience a fearless confidence in life? Why would this be a liberating choice? For some, it is obvious. Others may not yet understand the reaches of their choices. How we choose to live does not simply affect us; it also affects those we love.

Integrity is more than a high moral code. It is the ability to have the same values at play in every area of our lives. A business that is run with integrity, honesty, fairness, and transparency, as well as reliability and honor, has nothing to hide. The same is true of any person. Even if they are accused of lying, cheating, etc., a person of integrity has nothing to hide; therefore, the grounds of these accusations will not be found. May we be people who live by the values of Christ's kingdom in every area, unafraid of others' opinions and living for the Lord in it all.

A FRIEND IN DEED

Ask a friend for feedback about your character.

COMMON TEMPTATIONS

No temptation has overtaken you but such as is common to man; and God is faithful, who will not allow you to be tempted beyond what you are able, but with the temptation will provide the way of escape also, so that you will be able to endure it.

1 CORINTHIANS 10:13 NASB

When we are tempted, let's remember that it's not God doing the tempting. There are common enticements all around us, and these are part of the human experience. Even so, God promises to help us in our weakness.

Jesus resisted the temptations he faced in the desert with the Word of God and the Spirit as his helper. We can also use these tools to escape the lure of what we know is not beneficial. May we lean on the understanding and wisdom of God that clarifies how we should live and what awaits those who choose to follow in the ways of his kingdom. Some temptations will feel like our own desert experience. And with others, we can rely on the help of our community. Don't forget to reach out to trusted friends when you need perspective!

A FRIEND IN DEED

Ask for a friend's insight when you are struggling with temptation.

EVERYTHING COUNTS

Whether you eat or drink,
or whatever you do,
do all to the glory of God.

1 CORINTHIANS 10:31 NKJV

Nothing is too small before God. He sees every movement of our hearts and of our choices, and it all matters to him. Whatever we do today, let's do it for the glory of God. Let's do it to please him. He is not easily upset by us, so let's remember that we have liberty in love! We have joy in his fellowship!

Whether you meet with friends or family today, or you don't see anyone but strangers, may you approach every interaction with the intention of glorifying God. He is not looking for perfection; there is so much grace in his love. Let's lean into the presence of our God, praying unceasingly as we go about our day. Let's ask him for his perspective on the littlest aspects. Let's look to him through it all, for there is nothing too small. What matters to us matters to him!

A FRIEND IN DEED

Buy a favorite treat for a friend.

KEEP ASKING

> "Everyone who asks will receive.
> The one who searches will find.
> And everyone who knocks
> will have the door opened."

LUKE 11:10 NCV

Is there an area of your life where you have grown tired of waiting? Have you grown weary of asking the Lord about it? He meets you where you are, so if you are disappointed, he offers grace. He is kind with your desires, and he will continue to be faithful to his promises.

Do you have a friend going through this in an area of their lives as well? Perhaps you can pray for each other when you are too weary to keep praying for yourselves. Be beacons of hope for one another, holding onto the promises of God and interceding for each other. Don't stop knocking on heaven's door, for it will opened before you. Keep searching, for you will find what you're looking for. Keep asking, for you will receive.

A FRIEND IN DEED

Ask a friend what you can pray for them about.

RENEWED SPIRIT

"I will give them one heart,
and put a new spirit within them.
And I will take the heart of stone out of their flesh
and give them a heart of flesh."

EZEKIEL 11:19 NASB

Even when our hearts grow cold, we are not without hope.
God can take our hardened hearts and soften them in his
hands. He renews our spirits, refreshing our vision, and
bringing us to life in his love. There is no heart too far; no
person is out of the reach of God's loving and faithful hands.

No matter whether it is you that feels far from God
or if you're watching a friend walk through a time of
disheartened disconnection, take hope in the power of
God's love today. He is able to do far more than we could
ever imagine him doing. He is able to take hearts of stone
and turn them to flesh. As long as we are living, God is not
done pursuing us with his love—not ever!

A FRIEND IN DEED

Pray for a struggling friend to be renewed by the Spirit of God.

FAITH-FILLED PRAYERS

"I tell you, whatever you ask in prayer,
believe that you have received it, and it will be yours."

MARK 11:24 ESV

When we trust someone and they have proven their
reliability, we don't have to keep asking them to show up in
the same ways over and over again. When they listen to us
and do their part to make us feel heard, we probably feel
secure in that relationship.

God is faithful and true. He never changes. He is full of
loyal love today and every day. He is patient and kind,
slow to anger, and rich in mercy. How have we seen God's
faithfulness in our lives? How has he proven his character
to us? May we stand in the confidence of who he is and
believe that when we ask for what he loves to give, we will
receive it.

A FRIEND IN DEED

*Ask what you can do for a friend today,
and then follow through on it!*

BLESSED OBEDIENCE

"Blessed rather are those
who hear the word of God and obey it."

LUKE 11:28 NIV

Jesus said this in response to a woman who exclaimed that God bless Jesus' mother for birthing and nursing him. Jesus did not disagree that Mary was blessed, but he redirected the blessing to be accessible for all. Those who listen to the word of God and obey it are blessed by God.

Have you ever been in a situation where you felt heard by a friend in a conversation, and then later they demonstrated that they hadn't really listened to you at all? That can be an incredibly frustrating experience. Today, take time to really listen to the people in your life, and do what you can to communicate that you care about your connection. If they have talked about loving flowers, buy them some as a surprise. If they talk about wishing people would reach out to them more, make it a point to put a reminder in your schedule to text them often. Whatever it is, there may be a way to follow through and not just move on from your conversations.

A FRIEND IN DEED

Do something for a friend that you know shows love.

LEARN HIS WAYS

"Simply join your life with mine. Learn my ways and you'll discover that I'm gentle, humble, easy to please. You will find refreshment and rest in me."

MATTHEW 11:29 TPT

What wonderful promises the Lord Jesus gives us. He invites us to join our lives with his own and learn from him. As we unite our lives with his love and look to him as our wise leader, he reveals his patience, kindness, humility, and affection. There is rest and refreshment in his presence, for he is not hard to please!

Can you think of a friend who reflects these same values? Do you have friends who are easy to please and a joy to be around? They may not always agree with you, but even when they don't, you know how loved you are. What a wonderful gift they are from the Lord! No friendship will be perfect, but a true friend will be a delight to your soul more often than they are a challenge.

A FRIEND IN DEED

Think of a way you can offer refreshment to a dear friend.

FEARLESS TRUST

God is my salvation,
I will trust and not be afraid;
For the LORD God is my strength and my song,
And He has become my salvation.

ISAIAH 12:2 NASB

When God is our confidence, we have no reason to fear the unknown. The same God who saves our souls will keep us in his perfect peace even when troubles are near. Do we trust him to be our strength? Do we trust him to uphold us and keep us close as we endure the dark nights as well as when we journey through the bright days?

We can trust God because his nature proves faithful. Who do you trust in your life? Which friends have proven to be faithful through the ups and downs? Which ones have stuck with you through the feasts and the famines? Perhaps it has been a while since you have connected with some that come to mind. Take some time today to reach out and touch base with them. Even a short note can turn someone's day around.

A FRIEND IN DEED

Tell a friend that you are thinking of them.

TRANSFORMATIVE THINKING

Don't copy the behavior and customs of this world, but let
God transform you into a new person by changing the way
you think. Then you will learn to know God's will for you,
which is good and pleasing and perfect.

ROMANS 12:2 NLT

Have you ever tried to learn a new language? How about
spending time in a culture that is different than your
own? Without intentional practice and humility to try
to understand the worldviews or language differences of
others, we will not get very far in connecting with them.

Just as we can learn about the behaviors and customs that
are represented in this world, we can also become learners
of the culture of God's kingdom. How much time do we put
into learning the nuances of Christ's kingdom? As we give
our attention and time to becoming fluent in God's ways,
our minds will be transformed into the loving likeness
of our Savior. The more we learn, the more natural it will
become for us to live like he taught us to.

A FRIEND IN DEED

*Try to understand a friend's culture in a new way
by asking them questions.*

DEEP WELLS

With joy you will drink deeply
from the fountain of salvation!

ISAIAH 12:3 NLT

The waters of life are found in Christ. Jesus said this himself
when he spoke to the woman at the well and said, "If
only you knew the gift God has for you and who you are
speaking to, you would ask me, and I would give you living
water" (John 4:10). The living water Jesus was speaking of
was salvation.

We become wells of salvation, containers that bring the
living waters to others as God's sons and daughters. We get
to partner with God's heart and with Christ's purposes as
we share with others our joy and the power of God to save.
May we not forget the wonderful mercy that Christ has
shown us and the transformative power of his Spirit that
lives in us. Let's take time to share this hope with those we
interact with today.

A FRIEND IN DEED

*Share a specific delight that you have in the Lord
with a friend.*

REASON TO PRAISE

Praise the LORD in song,
for He has done excellent things;
let this be known throughout the earth.

ISAIAH 12:5 NASB

What has the Lord done that you are incredibly grateful for? Can you remember the last time relief and joy washed over you as you experienced an answer to prayer? Let that same relief and joy meet you again as you meditate on God's goodness both then and now. Let songs of thanksgiving rise from your heart to your lips.

We don't have to be in a church or in a religious setting to worship the Lord. We can offer him our songs of praise anywhere. Our hearts can sing love songs to the Lord as we go about our day, overflowing with praise even when we don't vocalize them. No matter how long or short it's been since we were overflowing with thanks to the Lord, let's spend concentrated time giving him praise from hearts of gratitude.

A FRIEND IN DEED

*Share an answered prayer with a friend
and ask them how you can be praying for them.*

DON'T COMPARE

God works in different ways,
but it is the same God who does the work in all of us.

1 CORINTHIANS 12:6 NLT

God's goodness is not offered to some and withheld from others. He is the same good Father to all his children. The work he does in our lives will look different because we are not carbon copies of one another. Have we learned to see the beauty in the unique ways that he meets us all? Just as a good and attentive parent meets each of their children in meaningful ways, so God does the same with us.

When we're caught up in the trap of comparing ourselves to others, we will come away either thinking too highly of ourselves or wishing for what others have. Pride or envy: these are pitfalls of constant comparison. Instead of measuring ourselves against others, let's measure ourselves against the truth of God's Word. Who does he say that we are? How is he moving in our lives and meeting us where we are? Let's lay down comparison and instead look for the light of God's love as it reaches us each in our own journeys.

A FRIEND IN DEED

*Tell a friend where you see God's goodness
shining through their lives.*

NOTHING FORGOTTEN

"Are not five sparrows sold for two cents?
Yet not one of them is forgotten before God."

LUKE 12:6 NASB

Have you ever felt overlooked, whether it be in a workplace, a church, or a friendship? We may feel small and insignificant at times, wondering if anyone actually sees us. Even when we feel utterly alone, we are not. God sees. He knows us through and through. There isn't a thing about our lives that is a mystery to him.

Let's lean into the love of God that reaches us in our uncertainty and press into the mercy that meets us in our vulnerability. God knows our hearts, he knows our circumstances, and he knows our hopes. Instead of waiting to be seen by those around us, let's show up as we are and reach out to those who matter to us. Not a single soul is forgotten by God, and when we turn our attention from our own insecurities to focus on what others may be experiencing, we are able to show up in compassion and freedom.

A FRIEND IN DEED

Ask a friend about something they shared with you recently, letting them feel heard and remembered.

THE COMMON GOOD

To each is given the manifestation of the Spirit
for the common good.

1 CORINTHIANS 12:7 ESV

No matter our gifts and talents, our strengths and places
of pride, we should use them all for the glory of God *and*
for the common good. Do we think about how we can use
the strengths we have in order to strengthen and encourage
others? Do we implement them in ways that serve the
greater good?

The Spirit ministers to us in our grief and brings us
comfort. The Holy Spirit offers us gifts that are meant to
be used to build up others and our own hearts in faith.
When was the last time we put these things into practice?
Have our lives become so focused on our own growth and
comfort that we have forgotten the importance of actively
serving others in love? Let's take this challenge and look for
ways to build each other up today.

A FRIEND IN DEED

*Volunteer to use your gifts for a cause you care about
and ask a friend to join you!*

STRENGTH IN WEAKNESS

Each time he said, "My grace is all you need.
My power works best in weakness."
So now I am glad to boast about my weaknesses,
so that the power of Christ can work through me.

2 CORINTHIANS 12:9 NLT

How much energy do you spend on presenting yourself as
doing well even when you are struggling? We don't have
to air our weakness for all to see, but it is important that
we are honest with those we trust. Have you shared your
struggles with a friend or two? Have you shown up as your
authentic self in your relationships?

God's power works best in weakness. His great grace
strengthens us. Do your friends come to you with their real
situations, sharing the weakest parts of themselves with
you? If you don't have anyone who does this, perhaps take
the first step of vulnerability with a trusted friend today.
Ask them how they are doing and be sure to share your
own reality with them. There is strength in weakness, not
only through the grace of God but also through the grace of
shared vulnerability and solidarity.

A FRIEND IN DEED

Have a deep conversation with a friend.
Make sure to carve out time and space.

PLAY YOUR PART

The body does not consist of one member
but of many.

1 CORINTHIANS 12:14 ESV

One of the important truths about life and relationships is
that we need each other. We need each other to thrive. Paul
describes the Church as being comprised of different parts.
Christ is our head, and we each play a distinct role.

Think of your friends. How differently are they wired?
What kinds of gifts do they have? What strengths do they
exhibit? Do you think one is more valuable than another
because of the role they have? Or do you see the value
in each? When we work together in unity, we are able to
support one another and accomplish much more than
we could on our own. Encourage the people in your life
to keep exercising their gifts, and do the same yourself,
knowing you bring value as well.

A FRIEND IN DEED

Share the value you see in a friend's gifts with them today.

STAY FOCUSED

Do not turn aside; for then you would go after empty things
which cannot profit or deliver, for they are nothing.

1 SAMUEL 12:21 NKJV

What are the driving values of your life? What are the most
important elements you can think of? Write them down
today, taking time to consider how they show up in how
you live your life. If one of your main values is cultivating
the relationships in your life, consider how much time you
give in your schedule to this. You can be creative in how
you choose to stay connected.

Spend some time focusing on what the weighty things of
life are for you: the elements you want to shine brightly
from your life to others. What do you want your friends
to say about you? What do you want to be known for?
Consider what needs to change in order for that to be true.
There is always room for refinement and fine-tuning. Let
intentionality lead you to transformation today.

A FRIEND IN DEED

*Ask a friend for their perspective
on what seems to be important to you.*

NEVER ABANDONED

The LORD will not abandon His people on account of His
great name, because the LORD has been pleased to make
you a people for Himself.

1 SAMUEL 12:22 NASB

No matter how far we feel from the Lord, he will never
abandon us. When we turn to him, we often find that he is
much closer than we realized. He has not left us to wander
on our own. Whenever we look to him, he is near. He is full
of help, and he will never leave us.

Do you have a friend going through a hard time right now?
Have you been a steady source of support for them in ways
that you are able to show? How could you demonstrate
that you are there for them even if miles separate you? At
the end of the day, the Lord's comfort is near and full of
healing, but our presence in the lives of our friends also
matters. We get to be concrete examples of the Lord's love
to those around us.

A FRIEND IN DEED

Let a friend know that you are there for them no matter what.

HONORING THE LORD

"Only fear the LORD and serve him faithfully with all your heart. For consider what great things he has done for you."

1 SAMUEL 12:24 ESV

How does serving the Lord faithfully affect your relationships? Are you better able to love those around you as you love God? If our relationships do not reflect the relentless mercy of God, then we may want to reconsider our idea of what honoring the Lord actually looks like. We are able to love others more fully knowing how fully we are loved by God. Let's first lean into his presence, asking for a fresh filling of his mercy, peace, and joy.

We are vessels of God's Spirit; he makes his home in us. From the endless source of his love, we can offer others the same mercy, grace, and peace that we are offered. We don't need to rely on our own resources when the Spirit of God is the well we draw from! Let's honor the Lord with all of our hearts, souls, and minds. Let's honor him through our relationships as much as anything else we do.

A FRIEND IN DEED

Offer a kind gesture to a new friend.

CHANGING TIMES

Since we are receiving a kingdom that cannot be shaken,
let us be thankful, and so worship God acceptably with
reverence and awe.

HEBREWS 12:28 NIV

Change is a constant. Perhaps we are flexible and ready to
move when the seasons shift. Maybe we resist change even
knowing that goodness comes with new beginnings. There
is grief in the letting go of old ways even when there is
excitement at the prospect of new ones. Though change can
be complex to navigate, the steady presence of God never
shifts or changes.

Have you experienced a shift in a friendship that is bringing
grief? You can take hope in the unshakable kingdom of
Christ without ignoring the pain of transition. You can be
thankful for what is coming and also be sad about what you
are leaving behind. Be gracious and compassionate with
yourself just as you would be with a dear friend. Look for
the gracious lining where gratitude resides and worship
God in the reality of your complex emotions. He can
handle it.

A FRIEND IN DEED

*Pray for increased grace for yourself
and for a friend who is going through change.*

STEP BACK

> "Do not keep striving for what you are to eat
> and what you are to drink,
> and do not keep worrying."
>
> LUKE 12:29 NRSV

Sometimes we get really focused on things that don't matter. When we get stuck in cycles of putting our energy into something that helps us feel in control but does not add lasting value, we are just spinning our wheels. Anxiety makes us feel out of control, so we try to latch onto things that seem important but make us feel worse in the end.

We do not need to keep striving for the simple things in life: what we will eat or drink or where we will live a year from now. Let's give God our worries about how our needs will be met and trust him to take care of us, so we can move forward and focus on what is ours to do. May we experience the relief of letting go even if we have to do it over and over again throughout the day. God is faithful, and he is worthy of our trust. He will take care of us.

A FRIEND IN DEED

Buy a meal for a friend.

LAY DOWN YOUR WORRIES

"People everywhere seem to worry about making a living,
but your heavenly Father knows your every need
and will take care of you."

LUKE 12:30 TPT

What are the worries that keep coming back to you? People
all around are worried about how they will provide for
themselves and their families, and this is not a baseless
anxiety. Jesus asks us to take our trust in the Father to a
practical level, to lay down our worries before him and trust
that he will provide what we need even when we cannot see
how it will happen. Trust does not demand details; it rests
in the character of the one in whom we put it.

How much do you trust the Lord? How convinced are you
of his goodness? Whatever your answer, God is faithful
regardless of your feelings on the matter. Why waste your
energy on worrying about what you cannot control? Lay
down what will never be remedied by your rumination and
let yourself rest in the peace of God.

A FRIEND IN DEED

*Offer to pray for a friend's worry
so they can let go a little more easily.*

WAY OF EXCELLENCE

Earnestly desire the greater gifts.
And I show you a still more excellent way.

1 Corinthians 12:31 nasb

Even though we are all given different gifts and talents, Paul says that we should desire the greater gifts. Why? Because it could benefit others. We already know that our gifts are not for us alone. What gifts do you desire? Which do you work at cultivating in your life and relationships? No matter what they are, keep going! And remember that above any gift, the *more excellent way* that Paul alludes to is living a life of love.

Whatever your gifts, how can you use them to communicate love to those in your family, in your friend circle, and in your greater community? How can you reveal the attributes of Christ's lovingkindness through the talents you already possess? May you be inspired by the Spirit of Christ within you in new and creative ways to live with love as your driving goal.

A FRIEND IN DEED

Use one of your talents to bless a friend today.

HUMBLE LOVE

Love is patient and kind.
Love is not jealous or boastful or proud.

1 CORINTHIANS 13:4 NLT

Read the verse for today until it sinks down deep, going from your head to your heart. Say it aloud. *Love is patient.* When we are patient with others, we practice the grace of God's love. *Love is kind.* When we choose kindness, beginning in our hearts and expressing it in our actions, we reflect the kindness of our Father.

Love is not jealous. Love has no need to envy others because it is not based on what we do or don't have. *Love is not boastful.* Love doesn't need to brag about how wonderful it is; love's merit stands on its own. *Love is not proud.* Love does not look at others and see where they fail. It does not perceive itself as better than any other. Love is unpretentious and humble. Give love freely with intention.

A FRIEND IN DEED

Practice patience in your interactions today.

AUGUST

It is good and pleasant
when God's people
live together in peace!

Psalm 133:1 ncv

FOLLOW HIS VOICE

You shall follow the LORD your God and fear Him;
and you shall keep His commandments,
listen to His voice, serve Him, and cling to Him.

DEUTERONOMY 13:4 NASB

How does following God affect the way you live? How does
it enrich your relationships? When we follow the Lord and
cling to his love, we obey his commandments, we listen to
his wisdom and leadership, and we choose to serve him.
When we put his wisdom into practice, we will find that his
ways are better than ours. His leadership is full of goodness
for us and for others.

How can you honor the people in your life in ways that
reveal the honor you have in your heart toward the Lord?
How can you choose mercy in your friendships today?
When Christ is your vision and focus, the shame and guilt
of former mistakes melts away. With clarity and peace,
you can offer others the purity of your compassion from a
grounded place.

A FRIEND IN DEED

*Ask the Holy Spirit to show you a way
you can serve a friend and then do it.*

NO RECORD

[Love] keeps no record of wrongs.

1 CORINTHIANS 13:5 NIV

Love does not hold onto grudges. *Ouch.* We are tempted by our pride to hold things against those who have hurt us. There are different levels of this to be sure. God's love, as large and pure as it is, keeps no record of wrongs against us. When we come to Christ, he cleanses us from all unrighteousness. This covers what we did with intention and what we did without even knowing.

Is there a grudge you've been holding against someone who has already apologized? Even in their efforts to make it right, can you just not seem to let go? Consider what it would take for you to truly forgive them. Can you take a step in that direction? Do you need to have a clear conversation with them, set boundaries, or simply choose to move on? Only you know what you need to do. Will you let love lead you forward today?

A FRIEND IN DEED

*If you recognize that you've hurt a friend,
reach out to them and seek to repair it.*

CULTIVATE CONTENTMENT

Be content with what you have, because God has said,
"Never will I leave you;
never will I forsake you."

HEBREWS 13:5 NIV

Contentment doesn't begin with what we do or don't have;
it begins in our hearts. Contentment is not something that
appears and thrives out of nowhere. It is something we can
cultivate within ourselves by putting certain practices into
place. When we take time each day to recognize the things
we are grateful for, contentment will begin to grow.

This does not only apply to our circumstances but also
to our relationships. When we begin to take notice of the
people we are thankful for, and we pay attention to what
they do that makes us feel loved, seen, and known, we grow
greater satisfaction in our relationships. Take some time to
consider those you are grateful for and why.

A FRIEND IN DEED

*Reach out to a friend you're thankful for
and tell them how much you love them.*

ENDURING LOVE

Love never gives up, never loses faith, is always hopeful,
and endures through every circumstance.

1 CORINTHIANS 13:7 NLT

What an incredible relief it is that love is not a limited
resource. It is expansive and ever flowing. There is always
more love to be had, to discover, and to draw from. The
Lord is the source of love, and he is always overflowing with
merciful kindness.

Have you ever had a friend who stubbornly stuck by you
in your darkest moment? Did they hold onto hope for you
even when you could barely muster any yourself? Did they
stick with you through thick and thin? This is love lived
out. This is the kind of love that our Father feels for us and
demonstrates through Christ. May we be friends who never
give up, never lose faith, are always hopeful, and endure
with each other through every circumstance.

A FRIEND IN DEED

*Thank a friend who has been reliable
and faithful through the ups and downs of life.*

KEEP CHOOSING IT

Love never fails.

1 CORINTHIANS 13:8 NCV

Does love ever grow old? Can love just die out? Scriptures say that love never fails. It never ends. The love of God is pure. Even though our own love may grow stale, it can be renewed in the waters of God's presence. He can revive the most hardened heart with the warmth of his mercy.

Have you grown tired of choosing love in any of your relationships? Consider why that could be. Is there a situation that feels utterly hopeless? Though people may fail us time and time again, the love of God never will. Let's drink from the fountains of his living mercy today and rest in the peace of his affection. With his love as our strength, we will be able to move forward.

A FRIEND IN DEED

Write a letter to a friend who needs encouragement.

FOREVER THE SAME

Jesus Christ is the same
yesterday and today and forever.

HEBREWS 13:8 NASB

Though changes in the world seem to happen at an alarming rate, there is one who never changes. *Jesus Christ is the same.* When we feel as if we have nothing to rely on, we can always count on Jesus to be the same; our merciful Savior and powerful Redeemer. He is the restorer of all things, and he is not finished working his miracles of mercy in the world or in our lives.

Change is not all bad. We are growing, learning, and evolving as we mature. There are a multitude of opportunities to begin again in the fresh mercy of Christ. Every day is a chance to choose how we will live. Will we live in the liberty of God's love? Will we pursue peace and uphold justice? Will we choose kindness, forgiveness, and restoration? Christ remains forever the same; let's keep transforming in his love and letting his example be our motivation.

A FRIEND IN DEED

Remember the things that have remained rooted in your relationships and express them to your friends.

GROWING UP

When I was a child, I used to speak like a child,
think like a child, reason like a child;
when I became a man, I did away with childish things.

1 CORINTHIANS 13:11 NIV

The more we mature, the more we understand what we could not when we were younger. How much more there is to learn! How much more there is to discover! Perhaps one of the most ironic traits of maturity is realizing how little you actually know. When we are young, we think we have a really good grasp on the world. As we experience more, we come to realize that there are factors at play that we previously didn't have a grid for.

It would be utter foolishness to discover a broader perspective as we mature yet refuse to adopt it. There are tremendous benefits to youth that we should not abandon. There is also incredible wisdom in maturity which we should not resist. How can we encourage each other in our growth instead of trying to stay the same at a foolish cost?

A FRIEND IN DEED

*Tell a friend the growth you've seen in them
and what you admire about it.*

IN THE END

Until then, there are three things that remain:
faith, hope, and love—yet love surpasses them all.
So above all else, let love be the beautiful prize
for which you run.

1 CORINTHIANS 13:13 TPT

When all is said to done, when we reach the end of our
time on this earth, three things will remain: faith, hope, and
love. These echo into eternity! Faith will be fulfilled, hopes
will be met, and love will never stop.

What is the one thing that defines your life? What is the
goal you are running toward? If it is anything but love or
one of its many expressions, take time today to consider
if it will be worth it when your time is up. What do you
want your friends to remember about you when you are
gone? Will it be how put together you were or how much
you loved them? Take some time to think through your
priorities and realign them if necessary.

A FRIEND IN DEED

Buy a gift for a close friend just because!

FRUIT-BEARING SPEECH

By Him let us continually offer the sacrifice of praise to God, that is, the fruit of our lips, giving thanks to His name.

HEBREWS 13:15 NKJV

Do your words encourage others? Do they reflect the hope, peace, joy, and love of the Lord? We don't have to perfectly represent God in our speech; there is so much grace for us. When we seek to honor the Lord, though, there will come times when we are challenged to do better because we know better.

What sacrificial offering can you make to the Lord through your words to others? Is it to practice more patience before you speak? Is it to offer more words of encouragement than you are used to doing? Is it to be clearer with your communication? As the Lord lovingly speaks over you as you spend time in his presence, ask him for grace to reflect that same love to others through what you say today.

A FRIEND IN DEED

Text a friend an encouraging note
and include what you appreciate about them.

OVERCOMING FEAR

"Don't worry or surrender to your fear.
For you've believed in God,
now trust and believe in me also."

JOHN 14:1 TPT

Jesus said this to his disciples on the same night that he
washed their feet and told them that the time was growing
close when he would not be with them any longer. Can you
imagine devoting your life to someone and then having them
share this news with you? Wouldn't you feel anxiety creep
into your heart as you thought about what it could mean?

Jesus does not promise that life will be easy or that we'll
get out of trials and trouble because of him. But he does
promise us his peace. He calls us to believe and to trust
in him. He calls us to overcome our fear by continuing to
believe his Word even through trembling. Overcoming fear
does not entail getting rid of it entirely but moving through
it with determination and faith.

A FRIEND IN DEED

Be a steady support to a friend
who comes to you with their fears.

THE WAY

"I am the way, the truth, and the life.
No one can come to the Father except through me."

JOHN 14:6 NLT

When we know Jesus, we come to know the Father through him. Jesus reflected the merciful heart of God the Father. Everything he did in the time of his ministry he was moved by the Father to do. Everything he shared he did so on behalf of the Father. In John 5:19, Jesus said, "I tell you the truth, the Son can do nothing by himself. He does only what he sees the Father doing. Whatever the Father does, the Son also does."

Jesus is the way, the truth, and the life. When we lose our way, let's turn to Jesus. When we are at a loss for what to believe, let's turn to his truth. When we are run down and weary, let's find renewed life in him. May we be a place of refreshing for our friends and point them to the one who can carry all their burdens.

A FRIEND IN DEED

*Unload your burdens on the Lord and ask a friend
if they need prayer for something specific.*

HOPE IS ALIVE

There is hope for a tree, if it is cut down,
that it will sprout again,
and that its tender shoots will not cease.

JOB 14:7 NKJV

If there is hope for a tree to sprout again and live after it
is cut down, then no matter what setbacks we face in life,
there is also hope for us! God is a redeemer; he takes the
ashes of our broken expectations and disappointments,
and he sows seeds of restoration. He takes our deepest
heartaches, breathes life into them, and renews our hope.
He is better than we can ever imagine, so let's not let
despair steal our hope in him.

Do you know someone who desperately needs to know that
God will bring life out of the circumstances which threaten
to break their hope? We all go through dark nights, often
brought on by deep loss, grief, tragic circumstances, or
trauma. But God is with us in the darkness, sowing mercy
into the soil of our lives even when we cannot see what he is
doing. Selah!

A FRIEND IN DEED

*Send this verse to a friend who is struggling to hope
and let them know you are praying for them.*

GIVE UP THE FIGHT

The kingdom of God is not eating and drinking,
but righteousness and peace and joy in the Holy Spirit.

ROMANS 14:17 NASB

Paul was addressing petty fights and debates that were happening among the believers in Rome. There were some who kept to strict diets based on the law of Moses and others who felt free to eat whatever they wanted to without shame. Though not needing to be a divisive issue, it had become one. Can you think of such an issue facing your church or the Church at large these days? Let Paul's words speak to that too.

The kingdom of God is not [fill in the blank with whatever issue you think of], but righteousness and peace and joy in the Holy Spirit. Righteousness, peace, and joy. These are what make up the kingdom of Christ. Are we too focused on issues that don't necessarily take away from Christ or his message but do cause us to withhold love and understanding from others? Then let's refocus on what the kingdom stands for and readjust our own opinions and reactions around that.

A FRIEND IN DEED

*If your opinions on a matter cause your friend to stumble,
avoid talking about that subject with them.*

HELP IN HIM

"The Helper, the Holy Spirit, whom the Father will send in
My name, He will teach you all things, and bring to your
remembrance all things that I said to you."

JOHN 14:26 NKJV

God is still working in new ways among us. He didn't stop
once Jesus was resurrected and ascended to his throne.
He didn't stop once the apostles had finished writing their
letters or after the Bible was canonized. The Holy Spirit is
an active teacher, a wise advocate, and his knowledge is
relevant today.

God is the same yesterday, today, and forever. We already
know this to be true. Our understanding of him may
change as we get to know his character better though. May
we never stop asking the Holy Spirit to lead us, to instruct
us, and to correct us. May we never stop pursuing the heart
of God to know him more and to be transformed by his
love. The Holy Spirit is our help today just as we can be a
help to those around us in practical ways.

A FRIEND IN DEED

*Remind a friend of a hope they shared with you
that they may have forgotten.*

A BETTER PEACE

"Peace I leave with you; my peace I give you.
I do not give to you as the world gives.
Do not let your hearts be troubled and do not be afraid."

JOHN 14:27 NIV

Have you ever come to a truce with someone, thinking you had put something behind you, only to find the issue resurrected a little while later? There may have been peace for a time, but it did not last, and in the end, it may have brought more trouble. It can feel like whiplash when peace is interrupted.

God does not give as the world gives. He offers peace to us for our well-being and in full knowledge that we could take it for granted. He doesn't offer us peace only so long as we behave. He offers us peace that is long lasting without threat of removal. His love made a way for us to be in restored relationship with him forever. If we stay away, it is not because he keeps us away but because we forget his kindness. May we let the peace that passes all understanding sink deeply into our consciousness as we turn to him today.

A FRIEND IN DEED

Send a gift to a friend who is far away.

NOT CONFUSING

God is not a God of confusion
but of peace.

1 CORINTHIANS 14:33 ESV

When we feel unstable in our relationships, it can be upsetting. We long for peace and harmony with the people we love, so how do we deal with it when it feels as though we just can't attain it? Let us start by going to the Lord who is full of wisdom and peace. He always has clear insight where we are at a loss.

Are we clear with our friends about our expectations, hopes, and disappointments? Do we take accountability for our reactions? May we communicate with clarity, not leaving confusing hints to be guessed at. Clear is kind. Let's stop playing games with the people in our lives; we cannot expect them to read our minds. Let's offer the peace of clarity for ourselves and for those we love. It benefits our peace of mind and offer others a chance to show up honestly themselves.

A FRIEND IN DEED

Have an honest conversation with a friend today.

DEFENDER

The LORD is my strength and my defense;
he has become my salvation.
He is my God, and I will praise him,
my father's God, and I will exalt him.

EXODUS 15:2 NIV

When our friends go through unexpected and prolonged times of trouble, how do we show up to support them? Do we offer practical help and encouragement? Do we keep showing up even if we don't know what to do? May we reflect the faithfulness of God in our dear friendships, offering ourselves as a steady support through the highs and lows of life.

God will never leave us in our time of need. Even when we fail, God will not. He is our strength and our defense. If all we have to offer is our prayer and love to a friend in need, let's make sure they know they have it. We cannot always physically show up—life does not always allow for it—but we can share with a friend that they are near in our thoughts and hearts.

A FRIEND IN DEED

*Let a friend know that you are praying for them,
and that God has not forgotten them.*

SEWN IN

"Remain in me, as I also remain in you.
No branch can bear fruit by itself;
it must remain in the vine.
Neither can you bear fruit unless you remain in me."

JOHN 15:4 NIV

We do not have to do life alone no matter how isolated we feel. The Holy Spirit is near, breathing hope, life, and peace into our hearts. He is our strength, our friend, and our leader. We can rely on God to get us through any and every circumstance, and he can minister to the parts of us that no one else can see.

When we remain in Christ, seeking his wisdom and his perspective every day, we foster the dearest friendship that we have: friendship with God himself! Let's give him time and attention today, asking for his input in our decisions and sharing what's on our hearts. Let's turn to him throughout our day. A better friend we could not find, for he is always close.

A FRIEND IN DEED

Thank God for the friendship of his Spirit.

EVEN FOR ONE

"If a man has a hundred sheep and one of them gets lost, what will he do? Won't he leave the ninety-nine others in the wilderness and go to search for the one that is lost until he finds it?"

LUKE 15:4 NLT

Jesus made it very clear that all are welcome in his kingdom. He did not spend all his time with the religious elite, and he did not shy away from being around those who were labeled as dangerous people to associate with. The religious leaders grumbled and complained about how Jesus welcomed sinners.

Are we more like the religious leaders of Jesus' day or like Jesus himself with our attitudes toward people? Do we reject the company of those who don't meet our standards? Or do we welcome all to our table? Let's lay down our biases in the light of God's mercy and allow him to transform our perspectives on people. Let's choose to keep open hearts and open minds no matter how different a person may seem. Everyone is deserving of kindness, respect, and opportunity.

A FRIEND IN DEED

Don't let pride keep you from pursuing friendship with someone different.

HOLY WISDOM

Whatever was written in former days was written for
our instruction, so that by steadfastness and by the
encouragement of the scriptures we might have hope.

ROMANS 15:4 NRSV

We can learn a lot from those who have gone before us.
Though the pace of the world may be different, the inherent
struggles we face are rooted in the same problems. When
was the last time you read something from someone who
lived before your time that challenged your heart in the best
of ways?

Let's not forget the benefit of the wisdom of our elders
in this life either. Do you have any friends who are
significantly older than you? If not, consider who the
trusted mentors are in your life. Who do you go to
for advice? Do you have an aunt or a father figure or
someone else you could spend time learning from? Let's be
intentional about asking the older people in our lives about
the lessons that they have learned along their own journeys.

A FRIEND IN DEED

*Reach out to an older person you respect
and ask to spend some time with them.*

SACRIFICIAL LOVE

"The greatest love of all is a love that sacrifices all.
And this great love is demonstrated
when a person sacrifices his life for his friends."

JOHN 15:13 TPT

Jesus said that the greatest love of all is one that sacrifices for others. If we claim to love others as Jesus loved, but it doesn't cost us anything, then we have room to grow. Love is not the easy choice. It is not the convenient choice. But it is always the best choice.

Think back to a time when you were a recipient of self-sacrificial love. It could have been from a parent, a friend, or anyone who sacrificed something in order to show up for you in a meaningful way. How did it affect you? May you be encouraged to love bigger, more intentionally, and at a cost when it counts. Look to Jesus. His great love was poured out even to the point of death. He knew what he was doing, and he empowers us to follow his lead of sacrificial love.

A FRIEND IN DEED

Sacrifice your time to be with a friend in need.

UNCONTAINABLE JOY

May God, the inspiration and fountain of hope, fill you to overflowing with uncontainable joy and perfect peace as you trust in him. And may the power of the Holy Spirit continually surround your life with his super-abundance until you radiate with hope!

ROMANS 15:13 TPT

Earlier in the book of Romans, Paul says that the kingdom of God is reflected in "living a life of goodness and peace and joy in the Holy Spirit" (14:17 NLT). The wonderful news is that we don't need to make this happen on our own. We can't conjure up the joy of the Spirit, but we can lean into his presence that is already overflowing and abundantly near.

Do you have a friend who whenever they are near, you find yourself being filled with the joy and peace that seems to overflow from their souls? The Spirit of God within them reaches out to you, and you can catch their enthusiasm. May we be the friends who are safe places to land, offering encouragement, peace, and joy just by being who we are.

A FRIEND IN DEED

Call a friend who brings you joy
and tell them how grateful you are for them.

CHOSEN

"You did not choose Me but I chose you,
and appointed you that you would go and bear fruit,
and that your fruit would remain."

JOHN 15:16 NASB

Just as God chose us in him, we get to choose our close
friends. We cannot be close with everyone in our lives, and
not every person who wants to be a part of our circle is
trustworthy with our most vulnerable parts. We should not
feel guilty about picking our trusted friends wisely, for the
quality of our relationships will affect our lives!

How intentional are you about letting your friends know
that you value their friendships? Perhaps it has gone
unspoken. Let today be the day that you express to a dear
friend how much you appreciate their presence in your
life. Tell them exactly what it is that you value about them,
and that you feel privileged to be privy to their lives. A
trustworthy and reliable friend is a gift indeed!

A FRIEND IN DEED

*Let a dear friend know what you value
about their friendship.*

WELCOME BACK

"He returned home to his father. And while he was still a long way off, his father saw him coming. Filled with love and compassion, he ran to his son, embraced him, and kissed him."

LUKE 15:20 NLT

The tale of the prodigal son is a story of the Father's heart of love toward each of us. Even if we abandon him, taking what he offers and squandering it, he does not hold our rebellion against us. When we turn to him, he closes the distance and runs to meet us. He embraces us and offers us the full compassion of his heart. What beautiful love! What liberating mercy!

When those we love leave us, may we keep compassion in our hearts for them. May we stoke the fires of mercy, practicing forgiveness. If ever they come back to us, may we welcome them with open arms the way our Father does. May we live out the same kind of mercy that we receive so abundantly from him.

A FRIEND IN DEED

If there is a friend you have been holding back from because of something in your past, take the first step toward reconnecting today.

OVERCOMING VICTORY

"O death, where is your victory?
O death, where is your sting?"

1 CORINTHIANS 15:55 ESV

Through Christ, we have victory over sin and death. There is the promised renewal of our bodies in the kingdom of Christ once we pass from this life into the eternal reign of his kingdom. We are free from the shame, the fear, and the blame of never-enoughs. We are fully restored by the overflowing love of our wonderful Savior.

Is there an area of your life where you feel stuck? Do you have relationships that seem to be in cycles that lead back to the same issues? Ask the Spirit for wisdom and seek out advice from those who can help. You are not bound by the threats of fear. No matter what you face, nothing is a death sentence, for you get to live in the liberated love of God that offers peace, joy, and rest.

A FRIEND IN DEED

*Offer encouragement to a friend who
is struggling with a hard relationship.*

BLAMELESS FRIENDS

Those who refuse to gossip or harm their neighbors
or speak evil of their friends.
Those who despise flagrant sinners,
and honor the faithful followers of the LORD,
and keep their promises even when it hurts.

PSALM 15:3-4 NLT

When we stand firmly in integrity, refusing to speak poorly about others, we reflect the steadfast love of the Lord. The kingdom of God is not full of slanderers but of people who choose what is right, what is merciful, and what is true. Let's not let the pressure of others turn us into people we don't want to become.

Do we keep our promises even when it hurts? Do we faithfully follow through on our word? Surely, we cannot be perfect. God knew this; he sent his Son, Jesus, to offer what we could not offer on our own. There is always room for restoration. Let's be people who don't speak ill of our friends or gossip about our neighbors. Let's keep our promises even when it costs us something. Let's be people of integrity, living for the kingdom of our Lord.

A FRIEND IN DEED

Speak highly of your friends to others today.

STAND STRONG

My dear brothers and sisters, stand strong.
Do not let anything move you.
Always give yourselves fully to the work of the Lord,
because you know that your work in the Lord
is never wasted.

1 CORINTHIANS 15:58 NCV

Whatever it is that you have been working for in life, do not give up. Sometimes the Lord will redirect you. Other times he will give you the strength to keep going right where you are. Lean into his wisdom and ask for his perspective today. If you are where you know you ought to be, don't let discouragement keep you from pressing into the work in front of you. Nothing you do is wasted.

This also applies to your relationships. The work you put into knowing, loving, and serving those around you is never wasted. There is no greater work than the way you show up for your friends and loved ones. Stand strong in your convictions and keep pursuing love. The Lord is with you in it.

A FRIEND IN DEED

*Encourage a friend who is weary, letting them know
that what they do is seen and it counts.*

LOOK BEYOND APPEARANCES

"The Lord does not see as man sees;
for man looks at the outward appearance,
but the Lord looks at the heart."

1 SAMUEL 16:7 NKJV

When the Lord looks at us, he does not judge us based on how well we are put together. He does not judge our looks; he sees straight to our hearts. He knows our insecurities, our motivations, and our hopes. He values what is in our hearts knowing it will motivate our actions.

Are we overly critical of people's appearances? Do we judge a person's worth based on what they look like? Or do we follow the loving leadership of our Father who looks beyond the outer appearance into the heart? How we treat others, how we speak about them and to them, and how we engage with the world will speak volumes more than how we look. Let's be people whose hearts are pure, who value others because they are expressions of God.

A FRIEND IN DEED

When you find yourself reacting to people based upon their appearance, connect to compassion in your heart and ask for the perspective of God.

TESTIMONIES OF GOODNESS

Oh, give thanks to the LORD! Call upon His name;
Make known His deeds among the peoples!

1 CHRONICLES 16:8 NKJV

When we are focused on the day-to-day, looking for signs of God's imprint on our lives, he will show us where mercy rises to meet us. We can cultivate hearts of gratitude as we learn to look for where his light shines on us in the simplest ways. We don't have to have a grand testimony of God's goodness to recognize that his goodness is present.

What simple, natural, and beautiful ways has God shown himself to you lately? Have you shared any of this with a friend, or have you kept it hidden in your heart? Consider sharing just one thing that has captivated you recently: how has God's tangible love encouraged your heart? You may find that verbalizing it to a friend encourages both of your hearts. No movement of mercy is too small.

A FRIEND IN DEED

*Share a revelation you have had of God's goodness
with a friend today.*

DIRECTED BY THE LORD

A man's heart plans his way,
But the LORD directs his steps.

PROVERBS 16:9 NKJV

As humans, we will make plans and follow through with them. This does not mean that the Lord is not in it. We don't need a sign from God to follow our hearts in life. We don't have to know with certainty which way we should go before choosing a path. We determine in our hearts which way we will go; this is our part. The Lord's part is to direct us as we walk it out. When our hearts are submitted to his leadership, he will guide us to the places best suited for us.

There is no reason to fear going the wrong way. Even if we were, God is more than able to bring us back. He is not afraid of our freedom, so why should we be? He has given us the ability to choose, and this does not mean that he leaves us if we choose something we really want. He is with us through it all. He directs our steps as we walk. We cannot know what the future will hold, but we know that the one who directs us is good!

A FRIEND IN DEED

Invite a friend along on a trip that you plan.

COURAGEOUS DEVOTION

Be on your guard;
stand firm in the faith;
be courageous; be strong.

1 CORINTHIANS 16:13 NIV

These words were a benediction to the church at Corinth: words of wisdom that Paul wanted to encourage them with. When was the last time you encouraged a friend with clear and decisive wisdom? When love and kindness are the motivation behind what we do, friends will know the sincerity with which we wish them the best.

Don't be afraid to speak words of encouragement. Don't be afraid to say the things that you wish someone would have said to you when you were in a time of transition or hardship. Let grace drip from your lips, letting your friends know how deeply you care about them and will support them no matter what. Don't tell them what to do, but encourage them to be strong in their convictions, courageous in the face of fear, and firm in what they know to be right.

A FRIEND IN DEED

*Ask God for a word of encouragement for a friend,
and then share it with them.*

SEPTEMBER

Love each other
with genuine affection,
and take delight
in honoring each other.

Romans 12:10 NLT

TRUTH TELLERS

"When the Spirit of truth comes,
he will guide you into all truth.
He will not speak on his own
but will tell you what he has heard."

JOHN 16:13 NLT

Who is the Spirit of truth that Jesus mentions in this passage? Is it not the Holy Spirit whom we have fellowship with here and now? We are not waiting for a far-off day to have access to the truth of God. Though we only see and understand in part, the Spirit continually guides us into all truth as we follow him.

Are you worried about a friend's journey in life? Do you wonder if the turn they've taken will lead them far from God? Firstly, know that you can be clear and kind with them. You can ask them questions about their life in order to hear how they got to where they are. Secondly and most importantly, you can trust the Spirit of God to guide them. If they are looking to him for leadership and help, know that the Lord can be trusted even if you would not choose the same path.

A FRIEND IN DEED

*Ask a believing friend what the Lord
has revealed to them lately.*

EVERY SINGLE THING

Let all that you do
be done in love.

1 Corinthians 16:14 NRSV

How different would our lives look if we chose to follow these words of wisdom? What if we intentionally went about our day choosing to show love in everything. When we wash the dishes, let's do it with love in our hearts for those that eat off the plates. When we run errands, let's have compassion on the people we interact with. When we work, let's have gratitude for the ability to earn a wage.

Love is a revolution; it will change us from the inside out as we continue to choose its ways. Love does not depend on reciprocation or valuation from another; it is something that we choose to extend. It is a gift given freely. It is vast, wide, deep, and high. It is the power of God! Let's choose to line our hearts, actions, and attitudes with love.

A FRIEND IN DEED

Be intentional about putting love into action today.

FULFILLING JOY

"Until now you have not asked for anything in my name.
Ask and you will receive, and your joy will be complete."

JOHN 16:24 NIV

It can seem like a big risk to assert your needs in
relationships when you are accustomed to denying them.
Does this ring true for you? Do you withhold your needs
in order to keep the peace or to not demand too much of
others? Are you fiercely independent, only asking for help
when absolutely necessary?

Maybe you have a friend who acts this way. When we learn
to suppress our needs early in life, we are conditioned to
think that we can only rely upon ourselves. However, there
is tremendous joy in asking for what we require, need, or
desire and giving someone the opportunity to meet us in
it. It is a vulnerable thing to do but so rewarding when we
receive what we ask for. Let's make more room for joy and
dare to ask for what we want in our friendships.

A FRIEND IN DEED

*Dare to be vulnerable with a trusted friend
and let them into your inner world.*

LOOSEN UP

"If you try to hang on to your life, you will lose it.
But if you give up your life for my sake, you will save it."

MATTHEW 16:25 NLT

Is there an area of your life where you are resisting inevitable changes? Do you struggle to let go of the hold you have on the idea of what your life should look like? Your resistance does not hold back time. It only makes the transition more painful for you. Can you ask God for help today in letting go in an area that you know you need to?

When we surrender to the will of Christ, we are immersed in his vast and gracious love. Though the path we tread in dark nights may not be what we would have chosen for ourselves, we are never without the comfort, guidance, and liberating love of God's presence. May we learn to let go of the things we could never control anyway and let the Lord of peace guide us into deeper healing as we trust him. We may just find the relief and freedom we have been longing for.

A FRIEND IN DEED

Ask a friend how you can help lighten their load today.

FATHER'S LOVE

"The Father himself loves you."

JOHN 16:27 NIV

The Father's love is not fickle or feeble. It is tender and strong. It is gentle and overflowing. It is all-encompassing and more vast than we could imagine. Let's not pass this moment by without meditating on the deeply passionate love the Father has for us. It is not wasted time or energy. It is our very life force!

Do you have a father figure in your life who has revealed the faithful and fearless love of the heavenly Father toward you? Has their impact in your life left you understanding the tender and passionate love of God more? Perhaps you have known the unrelenting love of a mother who never gives up on you. God is a good parent, and he reveals his heart through our surrendered lives no matter our gender or role. May we recognize the heart of the Father as it shines through men and women alike.

A FRIEND IN DEED

Reach out to a father figure and thank them for their love and wisdom that have impacted your life.

TAKE HEART

> "I have said these things to you,
> that in me you may have peace.
> In the world you will have tribulation.
> But take heart; I have overcome the world."
>
> JOHN 16:33 ESV

No matter what you are facing today, know that the Lord has not abandoned you. He is with you. Jesus already overcame the world, and we have fellowship with his empowering presence through his Spirit. His strength overtakes our weakness. His grace emboldens our hearts in faith, perseverance, and mercy.

The peace of God does not rest in only the good times. Jesus had just revealed what would happen to him, and then he shared this verse with his disciples! We can have peace knowing that God knows every bad thing that will come our way, and he gives us strength to walk through each one. His victory becomes our victory. His presence becomes our sustenance.

A FRIEND IN DEED

Remind a friend that God sees them where they are,
and that nothing surprises him!

GOODNESS OF GOD

Give thanks to the LORD, for he is good
his love endures forever.

1 CHRONICLES 16:34 NIV

Whenever we sense the goodness of the Lord, may we be in the practice of thanking him. Whether it's under our breath, in our hearts and minds, or out loud, let's not forget to give him gratitude. For those of us who know and follow the Lord, we can expect to encounter his goodness in our lives! In Psalm 23:6, David said, "Surely your goodness and love will follow me all the days of my life."

How expectant are we to be recipients of the goodness of God? Do we expect his love without his goodness? He does not give begrudgingly, barely offering us anything of himself. He gives abundantly from his love, and his mercy is everlasting. There is an overflowing fountain of delight in his affection, and we are the recipients of this unending love!

A FRIEND IN DEED

*Share with a friend how you have s
een God's goodness in your life.*

CHILDLIKE FAITH

Jesus called for the children, saying, "Let the little children come to me. Don't stop them, because the kingdom of God belongs to people who are like these children."

LUKE 18:16 NCV

Children, in their innocence and faith, do not have the chip on their shoulders that we do as adults. We may hear the gospel and balk at how good it seems; yet children are able to accept it more readily. If it doesn't sound too good to be true, it's not the fullness of God's love. Let's dare to believe God as children believe the dependable adults in their lives. He is a good Father to all.

Do you have a friend who comes to mind when you hear the phrase "childlike faith?" Someone who takes God at his word and can be overcome with wonder at the simplest things? This is not something to belittle in someone; may we join in the joyful awe that they carry with them wherever they go. Let's let go of our need to be mature all the time, learn to enjoy life a little more, and incorporate delightful innocence back into our lives.

A FRIEND IN DEED

Don't hesitate to talk to children about who God is.

GATHER IN FAITH

"If two or three people come together in my name,
I am there with them."

MATTHEW 18:20 NIV

When we've been in the habit of offering up our prayers on our own, we may have forgotten the power of gathering together and offering our united prayers in agreement with each other. There is encouragement and unity in praying for and with each other.

When was the last time you prayed with a friend? It can be an incredibly powerful experience, bonding together in the Spirit of God. Jesus promises that when we gather together to look to him, he will be there with us. Let's seek out opportunities to join together with other believing friends and cover each other, lift each other up, and advocate for each other as we lift our prayers to God. Even more, let's try to build it into our schedules for our spiritual encouragement and practice. The Lord will always meet us when we come together in his name.

A FRIEND IN DEED

*Carve out time to meet with a couple friends
and pray for each other.*

SOUGHT AND SAVED

"The Son of Man has come to seek and to save
that which was lost."

LUKE 19:10 NKJV

No one is out of the reach of Jesus. No one can escape the reaches of his love. Where we have lost hope for people in our lives to experience breakthrough, may we find our faith rejuvenated by the words of Christ. *The Son of Man has come to seek and save that which was lost*. He specializes in finding and restoring lost things and returning them to their rightful place in him.

Do you have a friend who is grieved over the choices of a loved one? Do you yourself feel this loss in your own life? Whatever the case, no matter how bleak it looks, God is able to do far more than you can imagine. Offer to cover your friend and their loved one in prayer. Dare to believe that Christ cares more for those we love than we ever could! Commit this verse to memory and repeat it when you find your faith waning. If the Lord can ignite a fire out of a damp offering and turn a heart of stone into a heart of flesh, he can move on behalf of our loved ones!

A FRIEND IN DEED

Pray for a loved one who is stuck in a harmful cycle.

INFINITE POTENTIAL

Jesus looked at them and said to them,
"With men this is impossible,
but with God all things are possible."

MATTHEW 19:26 NKJV

It is not possible for a person to save themselves. That's what Jesus was saying here. But with God, he says, all things are possible! What is impossible for us is not a hindrance for God. Nothing can stand in the way of his powerful mercy. When he declares us free in his love, then that is what we are.

Is there an area of your life or in the life of a friend where a wall is in your way? God makes a way where there is none, and he can remove the obstacles that we cannot shift on our own. Trust God in his faithfulness to do what you could never do. Pray big prayers, asking him to move on your behalf and on behalf of your loved ones. Trust that even when his ways look different than you expect, his lovingkindness will never leave you. His power to save is immovable. You will dwell with him in perfect peace and in the eternal joy of his kingdom!

A FRIEND IN DEED

Pray for God to move in situations that seem impossible!

ROCK OF REFUGE

My God is my rock.
I can run to him for safety.
The LORD saves me from those who want to harm me.

2 SAMUEL 22:3 NCV

God is a safe place of refuge to run to at all times. When we are overwhelmed, frightened, or threatened, we can run right into the peace of his presence. He surrounds us with songs of deliverance, as Psalm 32:7 says. He is our hiding place.

Do you have close friends who reflect this same kind of safety for you? Who do you turn to when life feels like too much and people make assumptions and accusations against you without really knowing you? A friend's comfort, their perspective, and their truth can ground us and remind us of who we really are when we feel as if the world is spinning. Let's always run to the Lord for refuge but let's not also forget to run to those we trust, those who know us and love us well, for encouragement.

A FRIEND IN DEED

Remind a struggling friend of their strengths,
their identity, and their worth!

SETTLED AND SUBDUED

"Is not the LORD your God with you? And has He not given you rest on every side? For He has given the inhabitants of the land into my hand, and the land is subdued before the LORD and before His people."

1 CHRONICLES 22:19 NKJV

When we know that God is with us, there is a quiet confidence that surrounds our hearts. His presence gives us rest even in the midst of the chaos. He settles our worries as he reminds us of his faithfulness and unwavering love. His power cannot be quenched, and he will not leave us to fight our battles on our own.

What have you fought for in life that the Lord has delivered into your hand? What areas do you see as blessings from God—even those that took time and energy on your part to receive? May your heart be encouraged as you start to see the thread of his marvelous mercy weaving through your life. Take this courage and perspective and share it with a friend who is in the middle of their own battle. The Lord God is with them just as surely as he is with you. He will also offer them rest!

A FRIEND IN DEED

Share a testimony of God's faithfulness
and peace in the midst of trouble with a friend.

FLIPPING THE SCRIPT

"Who is the greater,
one who reclines at table
or one who serves?
Is it not the one who reclines at table?
But I am among you as the one who serves."

LUKE 22:27 ESV

Though the rich and powerful of this world can pay others to serve them, this does not make them more important than anyone else. Money can buy you comfort, but it cannot buy your worth. Every person is valuable; everyone, no matter their status or class, is worthy of love.

Jesus did not come to be served but to serve. The King of kings—the one who was, who is, and who is to come—did not sit back and demand others wait on him. He took the role of a servant, washing his disciples' feet, teaching people from all walks of life the love of the Father and what his kingdom is like. He even went to the cross on our behalf. There is not a greater example of love to be found! May we find our purpose in how we can express this great love that is so freely given.

A FRIEND IN DEED

Pamper a friend who is struggling financially.

REFRESHING REFUGE

This God—his way is perfect;
the word of the LORD proves true;
he is a shield for all those who take refuge in him.

2 SAMUEL 22:31 ESV

Often, the thing we need most from our friends is not perfect advice, an itinerary for when we're together, or a gift of thoughtfulness. It's presence. We want them to be there. When we're happy or sad, celebrating or grieving, to have a friend there to be with us in it is what we long for. We can be comforted by the simplest of gestures.

Just as the Lord is a shield for all who take refuge in him, a good friend becomes a shield against the harsh aspects of life. Being with them can refresh us in our dry days, add even more joy to our celebrations, and make the most ordinary days more meaningful. Let's not forget the power and importance of showing up for our friends today.

A FRIEND IN DEED

Spend time with a friend.

COUNTED ON

God is not man, that he should lie, or a son of man, that he should change his mind. Has he said, and will he not do it? Or has he spoken, and will he not fulfill it?

NUMBERS 23:19 ESV

We all have people in our lives who we just aren't sure of their follow-through. Though we may love them dearly, reliability is not one of their strong suits. We may count them as friends still, but they are probably not the people we go to when we need support and action. What kind of friends are we? Are we people that our friends can depend on?

Let's be the friends that we want to have. Though no one is perfect, let's aim to be people of our word, following through on what we say we will do. Let's be more selective about the yeses we give so we have the capacity to carry them out. Let's be people who reflect the steadfastness of God in our relationships.

A FRIEND IN DEED

Follow through on a promise you made to a friend.

UNDERSTANDING

Then he opened their minds
to understand the Scriptures.

LUKE 24:45 ESV

Do you have any friends you share a deep faith with? Can you talk about what God is doing in your life, ask questions you have about the Word, and share what the Lord has been showing you? In fellowship with other believers, we can receive revelation through another's insight. What God speaks and reveals to others can inspire our own understanding and relationship with the Lord!

If it has been a while since you've been able to talk to someone about the questions, the revelations, and the other thoughts you have about your faith, reach out to someone who comes to mind today. We were created to build one another up in relationship, to encourage one another, and to challenge each other. We don't have to agree on everything in order to benefit from a relationship. In fact, where we differ causes us to grow outside our own experience and biases to see from a different perspective.

A FRIEND IN DEED

*Connect with a believing friend
and set up a time to have a conversation.*

WONDERFUL THINGS

LORD, you are my God;
I will exalt you and praise your name,
for in perfect faithfulness
you have done wonderful things,
things planned long ago.

ISAIAH 25:1 NIV

Have you ever had a grand idea of a way that you could bless a friend? Whether it was an idea for a gift, a trip to surprise them, or a fun way to spend a couple hours, were you able to implement it? Perhaps you had every intention, but time and priorities got away from you. Maybe you did, and it was wonderful.

Every plan and promise that God makes, he perfectly and faithfully follows through with. He does wonderful things! He hasn't forgotten a single promise. Take some time to dream with God about what you could do for a friend that would bless them. Make a plan, set up reminders and a timetable, and don't worry about how long it will take. Wonderful things sometimes take time, and that's perfectly okay!

A FRIEND IN DEED

Ask a friend what their dream birthday celebration would look like.

DEFEND THE HELPLESS

You have been a defense for the helpless,
A defense for the needy in his distress,
A refuge from the storm, a shade from the heat;
For the breath of the ruthless
is like a rain storm against a wall.

ISAIAH 25:4 NASB

God is a defense for the helpless and needy. He is a safe place of refuge from the harsh elements. He is a steady and enduring comfort to those who suffer. He never turns away a hungry soul. He doesn't require what we cannot offer. He simply bids us come to him.

How willingly do we do the same? Can we identify where we defend the helpless and needy? Do we advocate for those in distress, looking for practical ways to help them? Are we a safe place for those seeking shelter from the storms of life? Just as we go to God, may we be people who align with his values of compassion and mercy, offering respite and refuge to any who need it.

A FRIEND IN DEED

Make time to listen to a friend who needs to vent.

CLOSER THAN A SIBLING

A man of many companions may come to ruin,
but there is a friend who sticks closer than a brother.

PROVERBS 18:24 ESV

There is a saying that goes, "Friends are the family we choose." Though we cannot control the families we are born into, we do get to choose who our close friends are. Through time, shared history, vulnerability, and intention, we can become as close or even closer to our friends than we are with our blood relatives.

Do you have a friend who is like a sister or a brother? Are they as close to you as you can imagine being to anyone? Jesus is a friend like this: faithful and true. He never leaves, is always there when you need him, and he won't ever fail you. Let's continue to build trusted relationships with those in our lives who know us, see us as we are, and love us.

A FRIEND IN DEED

Send a card to a friend who is like family.

ABSOLUTE PEACE

Perfect, absolute peace surrounds those
whose imaginations are consumed with you;
they confidently trust in you.

ISAIAH 26:3 TPT

What would it be like to experience the absolute peace of
God every day? How would it change your perspective?
How could it change your relationships? God's Spirit is
accessible in fullness every moment of every day. You are
never without it, which means you are never without access
to the perfect, absolute peace of his presence.

Spend time meditating on the faithfulness of God today.
Spend time in prayer before you move on with your day.
Let your imagination run with the revelation of the Spirit as
you open your heart before him. Let the Word inspire your
prayers. Let your hopes drive your fellowship with the Lord.
Ask for his peace to cover and fill you and go forth into
your day with the peace of his presence that goes with you.

A FRIEND IN DEED

Look for ways to choose peace in your relationships today.

DO THE WORK

"Be strong and courageous, and do the work. Don't be afraid or discouraged, for the Lord God, my God, is with you. He will not fail you or forsake you. He will see to it that all the work related to the Temple of the Lord is finished."

1 CHRONICLES 28:20 NLT

It is not enough to be strong if that strength will not be tested. It means little to be courageous if you do not face situations that cause you fear. Let's follow the wisdom here as we face situations and people that cause us to question whether we've got what it takes. Let the strength and courage of God lead us to do the work that is ours to do.

This applies as much to our relationships as it does to the tasks we need to complete throughout the day. We have no reason to let fear keep us from moving forward in what we know to do. God promises to be with us. He will not fail or forsake us. He will faithfully see to the work that we have been called to do by blessing the work of our hands as we partner with him!

A FRIEND IN DEED

Ask a friend how you can help them move forward in an area where they feel stuck.

UNTIL THE END

"I am with you always,
even to the end of the age."

MATTHEW 28:20 NASB

Though the beginnings of new ventures are filled with
questions and unknowns, they are also filled with
excitement. As we move into the mundane middle, we may
have found more steadiness, but there is also a lot of work
to be done. Maintenance is not something that sounds fun,
but it is as necessary as the startup phase. We may lose
steam, but we must not lose sight of what is ahead if we
keep going.

As long as we are breathing, the Lord is with us—even to
the end of the age. He will not leave us in the mundane.
Is there a friendship that has become so comfortable that
you give it little thought? Does it feel as if you are in a
maintenance phase, showing up but not necessarily moving
ahead? Ask the Lord for his perspective and for his mercy
to shine a light on how this relationship can be refreshed.
He is a help in all things!

A FRIEND IN DEED

Do something new with an old friend.

PASSING THROUGH

We are here for only a moment, visitors and strangers in the
land as our ancestors were before us. Our days on earth are
like a passing shadow, gone so soon without a trace.

1 Chronicles 29:15 nlt

This life does not last very long. We don't know how many
years we get, and in the end, when our loved ones leave us,
it never feels as if it was enough time. This life is not our
final resting place. There is a promised life in the eternal
kingdom of Christ where there will be no more death, no
more pain, and no more sorrow. What a reality to look
forward to!

How does the brevity of this life affect how you relate to
those you care about? Have you had an experience with loss
that set your priorities straight and caused you to rearrange
your schedule? Relationships are the most important gifts
we have in this life. We cannot take anything with us when
we leave this life, but love lasts forever.

A FRIEND IN DEED

*Consider how you can give more time
to the important relationships in your life.*

FROM HIM TO HIM

"O Lᴏʀᴅ our God, all this abundance that we have provided
to build You a house for Your holy name, it is from Your
hand, and all is Yours."

1 Cʜʀᴏɴɪᴄʟᴇs 29:16 ɴᴀsʙ

Everything that we have in this life originates from the
Father. Every good thing is a gift from him! Whatever we
earn could not have been possible without the creation of
this world in the first place. May we hold it all loosely with
great grace and generosity. May we offer the Lord what is
his and be generous with those who have less.

There is tremendous value in setting aside a portion of what
is ours to offer back to God and to others. When we sow
into the communities where we live, with the resources
we have, everyone benefits. When we make giving a
practice and not a rare occurrence, we cultivate kindness
in practical ways. Let's choose today to be openhearted and
openhanded with what is ours.

A FRIEND IN DEED

Give an anonymous gift to a friend in need.

GRACIOUS LONGINGS

The LORD longs to be gracious to you;
therefore he will rise up to show you compassion.
For the LORD is a God of justice.
Blessed are all who wait for him!

ISAIAH 30:18 NIV

When it comes to the people we love, do we not long to be gracious? Do we not willingly show them compassion when we understand where they are coming from? Hopefully, we are not harboring bitterness, for that will surely lead to regret. The Lord is incredibly gracious and patient with us. May we also be gracious and patient with our loved ones.

Could we take this a step further as Jesus encouraged us to do, and not only be compassionate, kind, and understanding toward our friends, but also toward our enemies? Perhaps we don't think we have enemies, but if there are people we are withholding kindness from, we may want to look deeper and question why. Let's offer these people as much grace as we do to those we know and love.

A FRIEND IN DEED

Be gracious with someone who is upset with you.

ILLUMINATED PATH

Your ears shall hear a word behind you, saying,
"This is the way, walk in it,"
Whenever you turn to the right hand
or whenever you turn to the left."

ISAIAH 30:21 NKJV

We can trust the Lord to guide us through the twists and turns of life. Though we may not be able to see the path ahead of us, the Scriptures say we will hear his voice. When it is important that we turn, we will feel the leading of the Lord in that direction. When we submit to his leadership, we need never worry about where we are going.

Do you have a friend who is struggling to know which way to go? Are they stuck in place for fear that they will choose the wrong path? Send this verse to them today and pray for their peace of heart, mind, and body. Offer your wisdom if they ask for it, but more than that, just let them know that you are there for them no matter what. Even if they were to walk ahead and change their minds in the future, they can redirect! Encourage them in the grace of God.

A FRIEND IN DEED

Don't judge your friends' choices.

JUSTICE MATTERS

He is the Rock, his works are perfect,
and all his ways are just.
A faithful God who does no wrong,
upright and just is he.

DEUTERONOMY 32:4 NIV

God is not only merciful, but he is also perfectly just and
fair. He does not stoop to the laws and regulations of
this world; he is far above them! He sees what no eye can
perceive, and he knows what no mind can understand.
He sees every detail that we overlook and knows exactly
what needs to be done in order to bring restoration and
redemption. We can trust him to do it, even when we think
we know better. Guess what? We don't!

When issues arise in the world that divide families, let's
look beyond the extreme positions to where God is. Where
can we love one another and still stand for justice? Where
can we offer kindness and still stand on truth? There is so
much nuance in this world. We don't have to know what
God is going to do in order to align with his heart of loving
justice.

A FRIEND IN DEED

*When you disagree with a friend, choose to love them
while still holding onto your values.*

OASIS OF REST

He found them in a desert,
a windy, empty land.
He surrounded them and brought them up,
guarding them as those he loved very much.

DEUTERONOMY 32:10 NCV

Do you feel as though you are in a wasteland? Is it dry and lifeless all around? God comes to us in our desert seasons, and he surrounds us with his presence. He sows seeds of life and makes rivers run through the wastelands of our lives. Even where we cannot perceive life, where the Spirit of the Lord is, there is an abundance of promise.

The Lord guides us and keeps us like a shepherd does. He keeps watch over us, protecting us from enemies that we cannot see. He leads us through the dry land to a place of abundance and rest. He leads us to the still waters of his peaceful presence, and he offers us respite for our souls. When we see our friends going through hard times, we can also be places of rest; oases of refreshing for them!

A FRIEND IN DEED

Buy a weary friend a candle and some bath salts.

HOMES OF PEACE

"My people will live free from worry in secure,
quiet homes of peace."

ISAIAH 32:18 TPT

We cannot control how peaceful or chaotic others' homes
are, but we can add to the peaceful atmosphere of our
own. Whether we have children or pets, or we live alone,
we can add or take away things from our home to make it
feel comfortable, safe, and like our own space. Peace is not
defined by how quiet or loud the people are, or whether
toys are around, or the dishes are done. Certainly, this may
affect our minds, but it need not dictate the peace in our
relationships.

May we open our homes to those in our community,
whether friends, churchgoers, or neighbors. Let's figure out
how we can create spaces within the walls of our homes
that feel safe, secure, and a respite from the worries of this
world. Is your home a place of rest and comfort to you?
Is a friend's home a safe place where you can spend time
escaping the worries of life?

A FRIEND IN DEED

Invite a friend into your home.

OCTOBER

Above all,
love each other deeply,
because love covers over
a multitude of sins.

1 PETER 4:8 NIV

STEADFAST PURPOSES

The plans of the LORD stand firm forever,
the purposes of his heart through all generations.

PSALM 33:11 NIV

Even when people come in and out of our lives, there is one who will never leave. The Lord never changes his mind about us. Read that again. He never changes his mind about us! He loves us fully and completely, and his plan for restoration in our hearts and lives will not be deterred. He is merciful from generation to generation. He never stops moving in grace and drawing us in compassion.

Are there life changes or relationships that have ended in your life or in the life of a dear friend recently? Even when our plans fall apart, God does not miss a beat. He has not changed. He is still faithful. He is still full of wisdom. He has not abandoned us, and we can trust him to continue to guide us in his goodness. Let's trust him together.

A FRIEND IN DEED

Pray for a friend and ask one to pray for you!

SECURELY HELD

The eternal God is your refuge,
and underneath are the everlasting arms.

DEUTERONOMY 33:27 NIV

When life turns upside down and you don't know where else to turn, there is a refuge and safe space in the presence of God. As you turn to him, you will find rest. There is peace even in the unknowns and the tumultuous storms. He is like a walled fortress, keeping you safe. He is like a warm blanket, surrounding you with comfort.

The everlasting arms are underneath you, holding you up. They are there holding your friends too. Do you know someone who is going through an incredibly hard time? Are they struggling to keep their head above water? Offer them what you know you can, since nothing is too little, but also trust them to the care of the Lord because he will do even more. He will offer what you could not anticipate. He is so very good, and he will not let them go!

A FRIEND IN DEED

Be a support to a friend who is struggling.

OUR PRIME EXAMPLE

Be kind and loving to each other,
and forgive each other
just as God forgave you in Christ.

EPHESIANS 4:32 NCV

In Christ, we have forgiveness of all our sins, not just some of them. When we turn to him in repentance, he cleanses us from everything that once held us captive. He removes our guilt and shame. He covers our fears with his mercy. He is endlessly forgiving, never turning us away when we come to him.

How kind and loving are we to the people in our lives? When Peter asked how many times he should forgive those who hurt him, did Jesus respond with only a few? No. He replied that he "must forgive him even if he wrongs you seventy times seven" (Matthew 18:22). When a fellow believer wrongs us, we have no excuse to harbor bitterness against them. Forgiveness is freedom, as much for us as it is for them!

A FRIEND IN DEED

*Release a grudge you've been holding
and forgive someone for the wrong they've done.*

SLOW TO ANGER

"The LORD, the LORD,
a God merciful and gracious,
slow to anger,
and abounding in steadfast love
and faithfulness."

EXODUS 34:6 NRSV

The more our hearts heal, the more time we spend with the Lord in his Word and in his presence, the more like him we become. His values become our own. His characteristics begin to shine through as we align with his kingdom ways. God, who is merciful and gracious, who is slow to anger and abounding in love and faithfulness, transforms us continually into his image as we look to him in all we do.

If we easily become frustrated, it is a sign of our misaligned expectations and neglected needs. God is perfect, and he is patient and slow to anger. Just because we experience frustration, irritation, or anger, it does not mean that we are sinning. It means that there is something lying underneath those things. Before we lash out, let's ask ourselves: why do I feel so strongly about this?

A FRIEND IN DEED

*If you feel angry toward someone today,
ask yourself what lies underneath that feeling.*

HE IS COMING

Say to those with fearful hearts,
"Be strong, and do not fear,
for your God is coming to save you."

ISAIAH 35:4 NLT

We cannot escape the feeling of fear in our lives. It is hardwired into our nervous systems. There will be circumstances and situations where fear will rise up. We were created with emotions, and fear is one of them! It is like an alert system. Even so, in our fear, let's stay grounded in the love and steadfast mercy of God. He never changes. Courage and strength rise up as we face our fears, not as they disappear.

Our God is trustworthy and faithful. He will save us even from the things we cannot anticipate or escape. He is our peace, our redemption, and our help. Let's trust him to do what we cannot, and let's continue to follow him with faith and courage. Fear may try to keep us stuck, but leaning on God's help will empower us to move forward in courageous perseverance.

A FRIEND IN DEED

*Share a testimony of God's faithfulness
with a friend who is facing a lot of fear.*

GATHERED IN

He takes care of his people like a shepherd.
He gathers them like lambs in his arms
and carries them close to him.
He gently leads the mothers of the lambs.

ISAIAH 40:11 NCV

God is a shepherd to *all* who look to him. No matter the
stage of life we find ourselves in, no matter how many
people we are responsible for, God is faithful to guide us and
to keep us. He gathers us in like little lambs in his arms. He
gently leads the mothers. He directs even the stubborn with
his staff and goes off to find the sheep who wander away.

No matter how alone we feel, there is a flock we belong to.
There are people we are meant to connect to and gather
together with. We do not have to be the same to be united
in purpose. We do not have to have similar lifestyles to be
loving and supportive. We don't have to believe all the same
things in order to prioritize mercy, justice, and peace. Let's
follow the Shepherd where he leads us and trust him to
gather us into the fold of his flock.

A FRIEND IN DEED

*Connect more deeply with the people who are a part of
your life whether you naturally feel close to them or not.*

CALLED BY NAME

Lift up your eyes on high
And see who has created these stars,
The One who leads forth their host by number,
He calls them all by name.

ISAIAH 40:26 NASB

When was the last time you were out in a secluded place on a dark, clear night? When we get away from the light pollution of large cities, we can see what remains hidden in the glow of city lights. Out where the stars shine bright and you can see clusters of tiny stars hidden among the brighter constellations, it's hard not to feel the wonder of the Creator.

Scripture says that God calls out the names of each star, and there are multitudes! If he knows the name of each burning rock in the sky, how much more does he know and call out our names? He who placed the stars in the sky is the same one who knit us together, who lovingly created us each in his image. What a wonderful and awesome truth this is!

A FRIEND IN DEED

Treat every person you meet as the wonderful creation they are.

HE DOES NOT WEARY

Do you not know? Have you not heard? The LORD is
the everlasting God, the Creator of the ends of the earth.
He will not grow tired or weary, and his understanding
no one can fathom.

ISAIAH 40:28 NIV

Even when we have absolutely nothing left to give, God is
full of grace. He is full of strength. He does not waver nor
grow weary. He is as alert and compassionate, as ready to
help and full of wisdom, as he ever was or will be. Though
we may tire easily, God never does.

What are you or a friend facing that feels overwhelming
today? Does hopelessness gnaw at your heart or mind? May
you turn from your own discomfort and give it to the Lord
who remains constant through it all. He is actually that
good! He is that trustworthy! He is that strong! Trust him.

A FRIEND IN DEED

Share today's verse with someone who needs to hear it.

STRENGTH TO THE TIRED

He gives strength to those who are tired
and more power to those who are weak.

ISAIAH 40:29 NCV

When our friends or loved ones are dealing with sickness
that zaps their energy, it can be hard for everyone.
Their own expectations and abilities may be hampered.
Our inability to help or fix what is wrong may leave us
discouraged. Even in the face of overwhelming odds, God
is faithful to strengthen us in his presence.

Instead of trying to fix what is wrong, can we show up and
accept where they are and love them through it? Let's ask
them what would make them feel loved and supported, and
then let's respect and honor their answers. The love of a
friend can bring relief and joy. Simple solidarity can breed
strength in the most exhausted heart. We don't have to have
all, or even any, answers. Let's show up in kindness and
compassion with open hearts.

A FRIEND IN DEED

Ask a worn-out friend what would bring relief to them.

RENEWED IN THE WAITING

Those who wait for the LORD shall renew their strength,
they shall mount up with wings like eagles,
they shall run and not be weary,
they shall walk and not faint.

ISAIAH 40:31 NRSV

Few of us enjoy the waiting periods in life. When we have an idea of what we want, whether we are working toward it or waiting our turn in line, it is an act of perseverance and patience to keep holding onto hope without dictating the timeframe. God is not on our timeline. He takes into consideration things that we cannot even fathom. We can trust his goodness and his faithfulness.

Let's not give up hope for our own waiting and let's encourage our friends in theirs. We can accept what is available to us at the moment and lean on the wisdom and strength of God to meet us whenever we need it. He is more than able to refresh us when our hearts grow weary and to strengthen us when we are tired.

A FRIEND IN DEED

Treat a friend to a nice coffee or meal today.

FEAR NOT

"Don't be afraid, for I am with you.
Don't be discouraged, for I am your God.
I will strengthen you and help you.
I will hold you up with my victorious right hand."

ISAIAH 41:10 NLT

What circumstances are you facing that cause worry and fear to creep up? When we find ourselves in seasons that look nothing like we hoped our lives would look, it becomes a daily practice to lay down our expectations. Jesus is always a safe place to unburden our hearts. He is a refreshing place of peace even in the midst of troubles and unforeseen trials.

How can you implement courage today, not only when it comes to what you do, but also in how you interact with others? Is there someone that you've hesitated to have an honest conversation with, but you know it needs to be had? Let today be the day you lean on the strength of God to empower you. Have the vulnerable conversations, be open, and lean on God in the unknown of it all.

A FRIEND IN DEED

Have a conversation you've been avoiding having.

UNSTOPPABLE

*"I know that you can do anything,
and no one can stop you."*

JOB 42:2 NLT

When we lose focus of who God is and let our circumstances overwhelm our faith with fear, we can feel displaced and completely in despair. But when we listen to the Lord, remembering who he is and how powerful he is, our perspectives are rightly shifted. Job had an encounter with God that shifted his perception of his troubles, and in the end, he put his faith back in God.

Is there an area of your life that feels outside of God's grace? Know that the Lord in his wisdom has not forgotten you. He has not left you to waste away. He is full of wisdom, and he is ready to restore you with peace. Let the unstoppable God overwhelm your worry with his faithfulness, for he never ever changes. Take some time to listen to what God is saying to you today; he is full of mercy and truth.

A FRIEND IN DEED

*Humble yourself before others when you are wrong
and admit your change of heart.*

PLACE OF BELONGING

"I have redeemed you;
I have called you by name;
you are Mine!"

ISAIAH 43:1 NASB

Even when we feel disconnected from our friends, there is a place of belonging, a home base that never wavers. The Lord who has redeemed us calls us by name. We belong to him! And those who belong to the Lord also belong to each other. Where have you pulled away from relationships that could actually benefit you?

As you belong in the kingdom of God, so do you belong in his family. If you are coming out of a time of isolation, reach out with intentionality to those who you have known to be safe and trustworthy people in your life. You don't have to put yourself out there for everyone in the same way. Come back home to those who make you feel seen, known, and loved just for being yourself. The ones who have loved you and accepted you the way you are a safe landing.

A FRIEND IN DEED

Reach out to an old friend you haven't spoken to in a while.

IRREVERSIBLE MERCY

"Even from eternity I am He,
and there is none who can deliver out of My hand;
I act and who can reverse it?"

ISAIAH 43:13 NASB

No one can stop the mercy of God. Nothing can get in its way: not wars, nor famines, nor floods. No storms, nor fires, nor deep freezes can keep his love at bay. When God moves, nothing can stop him. What areas of your life need a fresh infusion of his faithful mercy? Where do you need his kindness to meet you?

When we choose the intention of compassion in our interactions, though fear or misunderstanding or offense may try to dissuade us, may we remain faithful to follow through with love. It is not dependent on others' reactions. If God is love and we are in him, then we get to move in his love without the need to control how it will be received. Let's follow the lead of our merciful Savior and walk in his steps on the path of laid-down love.

A FRIEND IN DEED

*Choose compassion in your interactions today
no matter the mood of anyone you meet.*

BEAUTY OUT OF ASHES

"I am about to do something new.
See, I have already begun! Do you not see it?
I will make a pathway through the wilderness.
I will create rivers in the dry wasteland."

ISAIAH 43:19 NLT

God is wonderful at creating, not only in the beginning but in every moment. The universe is constantly expanding. How much more, then, is the love of God? God is always up to something new. No matter what endings we have faced, there is more opportunity ahead of us. The Lord meets us with abundant grace wherever we find ourselves.

Do you need a fresh dose of hope today? Do you know a friend who does? May your encouragement lead you to sharing it with others. Where you have felt stuck and at a loss for what to do or where to go, may you feel the Lord's strong hand guiding you through an open door to his goodness. He is not finished sowing seeds of glory in your story!

A FRIEND IN DEED

Share a hope you have with a friend
and ask them about one that they carry.

GUILT IS GONE

"I have swept away offences like a cloud,
your sins like the morning mist.
Return to me, for I have redeemed you."

ISAIAH 44:22 NIV

Have you ever felt tension in a relationship, and it caused you to pull away from the other person? Perhaps you felt as if you failed and the guilt you feel about disappointing them has kept you from reaching out. Maybe you have felt like something is bothering them, and you assume it must have been something you did. Instead of letting guilt keep you from your friendships, let the grace of God meet you and empower you to connect in humility and vulnerability today.

God has removed our guilt from us. What a wonderful Father! Do we also give the friends in our lives an opportunity to receive us when we come to them in humility? Let's seek restoration when we have messed up. Let's let go of the guilt that perfectionism brings and instead show up in our weak humanity. A good friend will receive us when we do.

A FRIEND IN DEED

*Take a step to reconnect with a friend
you have felt estranged from.*

HIDDEN TREASURES

"I will give you hidden treasures,
riches stored in secret places,
so that you may know that I am the LORD,
the God of Israel, who summons you by name."

ISAIAH 45:3 NIV

There is more treasure found in the wisdom of God than any we could accumulate in this world. The kingdom of heaven is full of costly riches, some of which we can experience now through fellowship with the Spirit. This is not a prosperity gospel; it is the incomparable fruit of God's Spirit. There is an abundance of love, joy, peace, patience, kindness, and so much more in him. These things are more lasting and more satisfying than gold or silver!

What hidden treasures can you offer the friends in your life through relationship with you? Do they find patience, peace, and compassion? Are they met with kindness and understanding? How about encouragement and hope? Keep prioritizing your fellowship with God's Spirit and watch how it revitalizes and reflects on your earthly relationships.

A FRIEND IN DEED

*Choose a fruit of the Spirit to focus
on practicing in your relationships today.*

COMFORT FOR SUFFERING

Sing for joy.
For the Lord has comforted his people
and will have compassion on them in their suffering.

Isaiah 49:13 NLT

Have you bought into the idea that a godly life is a pain-free life? Do you believe the lie that if someone is suffering, then they brought it upon themselves? Surely our choices reflect in some of our circumstances, but some things just happen. Suffering is inevitable in life. We will all walk through grief and sorrow, and not one of us will escape it.

Jesus doesn't promise that he will save us from our suffering. He promises to be with us in it. This is extremely good news! When troubles come, he does not leave us. When pain cuts us deeply, he is our healing presence and our peacekeeper. He comforts us in our sorrow, and he has compassion on us in our suffering whether we brought it upon ourselves or not.

A FRIEND IN DEED

Buy a cozy blanket for a friend who is suffering.

RISE UP IN CONFIDENCE

The LORD God helps me,
Therefore, I am not disgraced;
Therefore, I have set my face like flint,
And I know that I will not be ashamed.

ISAIAH 50:7 NASB

When we know that someone has our back, it gives us confidence to move courageously forward. Have you ever had the experience of needing to start something new and potentially overwhelming, but the support of your friends gave you the confidence you needed to push through? The encouragement and support of people who love us, are for us, and are in our corner cannot be overstated.

If you have a friend going through a hard transition, reach out to them today with intention. Encourage them, reminding them of who they are and the strengths they possess. Be there for them when they need a dose of fresh courage and cheer them on. Show up for your people and stand with them. Then watch them rise up in confidence!

A FRIEND IN DEED

Help a friend who needs a fresh dose of encouragement.

HUMBLE HEARTS

My sacrifice, O God, is a broken spirit;
a broken and contrite heart you, God, will not despise.

PSALM 51:17 NIV

God never turns away a humble and repentant heart. A good friend won't either. When friends come seeking restoration, let's offer them the same kindness that we receive in Christ. Let's receive them with compassion and bless them with forgiveness. There are some hurts that require us to keep our distance. Abuse should not be excused, and we should not reenter situations where we are subject to it. However, we can still offer forgiveness without giving them access to hurt us again.

In other cases, we may find forgiveness easy. When we love someone, we want to be connected and restored. May we apologize to those we hurt when we recognize that we've done so. May we not let pride keep us from admitting our faults. Let's remain humble in love and open in compassion.

A FRIEND IN DEED

Let go of an offense you have been carrying against someone.

TO BE KNOWN

"I want you to show love,
not offer sacrifices.
I want you to know me
more than I want burnt offerings."

HOSEA 6:6 NLT

It is a basic human desire to be known. It's important to know that this doesn't start with us. God himself wants us to know him more than he desires our offerings and sacrifices. He wants us to know him, just as we long to be known. He wants us to understand who he is—his heart and character—in the same ways that we want to be understood. Our longing to be seen reflects the desire of God's heart.

How much time do we give to our friendships, not only in doing things together but in discovering the heart of those we are in relationships with? It takes time, attention, and intention to get to know someone well. The beautiful thing about relationships is that we are ever changing, so there's always more to discover! Let's make time to discover new things about our friends as we ask deeper questions and pay attention to how they show up in our lives.

A FRIEND IN DEED

Carve out time to connect with a friend in deep conversation.

THROUGH EVERYTHING

"Though the mountains be shaken
and the hills be removed,
yet my unfailing love for you will not be shaken
nor my covenant of peace be removed,"
says the LORD, who has compassion on you.

ISAIAH 54:10 NIV

No matter what unexpected thing crops up in our lives, no matter how terrifying the situation may be, God promises that his peace will not be removed. He has offered us the abundance of his unfailing love through every heartache and trauma. Though the mountains shake and the hills be removed, God remains constant in mercy.

When our lives are shaking, may we cling to the Rock that is greater than we are. He is the immovable foundation beneath our feet. His love is unbreakable. However many times it takes to redirect our focus to his steadfast presence, let's do it. Let's keep looking to the lover of our souls who never leaves. He is full of compassion, grace, and wisdom, and he always will be.

A FRIEND IN DEED

Tell a friend who is going through
a terrible time that you love them.

LED OUT IN PEACE

You will go out with joy and be led out in peace.
The mountains and hills will burst into song before you,
and all the trees in the fields will clap their hands.

ISAIAH 55:12 NCV

When we look to the Lord as our leader, following his ways and being transformed in his living love, it is his joy and peace that go before us. Where the Spirit of the Lord is, there is freedom. Where there is freedom, there is joy. Where there is liberty, there is peace. No matter what may be going on in the world around us, when the Lord loves us to life in his presence, there is unspeakable delight and reviving for our souls.

When our friends come out of hard times and enter into new, spacious places in life, relationships, work, etc., do we not rejoice with them? Let's not hold back our celebration for our loved ones' breakthroughs! It is good to gather together and honor beautiful new beginnings. Let's lead our friends out in peace and join with their joy!

A FRIEND IN DEED

Celebrate a friend's success with them,
no matter how small.

WELL-WATERED GARDENS

You will be like a well-watered garden,
like a spring whose waters never fail.

Isaiah 58:11 NIV

Without tending, gardens will grow wild. Vines may thrive while they choke the life out of more delicate plants. The Lord tends to us with care and attention. He is wise in his pruning, knowing what needs to be cut away in order for new life to bloom. Do we trust him in the painful trimming?

Just as a well-watered garden will thrive, so will well-watered relationships. What we give care, time, and attention to, will grow. Let's be proactive in our friendships, making the necessary adjustments. Let's make room in our schedules to water the relationships in our lives. A neglected friendship will have the same issues as a neglected garden. But we can get to work and put the pruning shears to it by cutting away our pride and humbling ourselves in vulnerability.

A FRIEND IN DEED

*Schedule time for your dear friends
and make it a regular occurrence.*

DIVINE EXCHANGE

I will give them a crown to replace their ashes,
and the oil of gladness to replace their sorrow,
and clothes of praise to replace their spirit of sadness.

ISAIAH 61:3 NCV

No dark night lasts forever. Morning comes, and with it the rising of the sun. Light shines and dissipates the shadows. We see clearly what we could not perceive with our eyes in the pitch black. We might have felt alone in our sorrow, but when relief comes, perhaps we can see where mercy was already with us.

God is great at giving us his goodness in exchange for our barrenness: his strength for our weakness, his love for our fears, his peace for our worries, his joy for our sorrow. He will never fail to reach out to us in loyal love. Never. Wouldn't we do whatever we could for our loved ones to thrive? Wouldn't we offer them all the good we have in order to help them through their hardships? God is the same. In fact, he is so much better! He is perfect in love, and he will never change.

A FRIEND IN DEED

Buy a friend something new to replace what has worn out.

ALWAYS WORKING

From ages past no one has heard,
no ear has perceived,
no eye has seen any God besides you,
who works for those who wait for him.

ISAIAH 64:4 NRSV

God is greater than we can understand. He is outside of our scope of understanding, so much more wonderful, so much more vast, so much more powerful than we could ever imagine. He is capable of far more than we could visualize. He is full of truth and mercy, and he is unflinchingly faithful.

Sometimes, all we need is a reminder of this truth: God is always working for those who wait for him. All who look to him will be satisfied. All who open their hearts to him will experience his peace. We cannot know all the pieces that fit together in his hand. But we can trust him in his kindness to follow through on everything he said he would. He is good, he is trustworthy, he is alert, and he is moving.

A FRIEND IN DEED

*When a friend shares a hope they have with you,
believe in it with and for them.*

ETERNAL PORTION

My flesh and my heart fail;
But God is the strength of my heart
and my portion forever.

PSALM 73:26 NKJV

Even when our health and mind and our heart give up, God remains the same. He is our perfect portion in our health and in our sickness. In our weariness and in our strength, God is our eternal hope. Good friends reflect the steadfastness of God, and no matter what we are going through or how well we show up, they remain loving, kind, and true.

Who has been a loyal friend to you? Who has been there to celebrate your successes and support you in your failures? Who has loved you through the hard times as well as the good? We don't have to agree with everything about our friends' opinions and choices to show up in loyal love. Hopefully, we already know this and practice it. But if we need this reminder today, let's seize the opportunity to let love speak for itself.

A FRIEND IN DEED

Thank a faithful friend for their love and support.

SHEPHERDED BY LOVE

Know that the Lord Himself is God;
It is He who has made us, and not we ourselves;
We are His people and the sheep of His pasture.

PSALM 100:3 NASB

As you look ahead to the unknowns of the future, do they overwhelm you, or do you feel at peace? Perhaps it's a mixture of both. Whatever comes, the one who created you goes with you. Nothing surprises him, and he cannot be overcome by fear. Give him your worries today as you meditate on his presence with you. He is larger than your little life, and he will not fail you.

Just as your good Father shepherds you, so does he guide all those who look to him. You don't have to worry about your friends or their choices. You don't have to try to control which direction they go. You are not responsible for anyone else's choices, and that is actually really good news! Lay down your criticism of others' paths and instead trust them to the Good Shepherd.

A FRIEND IN DEED

*Love your friends where they are no matter how much
you disagree with their choices.*

ALWAYS READY

The Lord is always good and ready to receive you.
He's so loving that it will amaze you—
so kind that it will astound you!

PSALM 100:5 TPT

There is so much goodness, so much richness in this passage of Scripture. It is a privilege to worship this God as the psalmist declares earlier in the chapter, "For he is our Creator and we belong to him. We are the people of his pleasure" (v. 3). The Lord is always ready to receive us when we turn to him—every single time. Let's not hesitate to run into his astoundingly kind arms today.

Are we always ready to receive our friends who turn to us? We are not God, and we cannot do this perfectly, but we can certainly make it our aim to show up in kindness and receive those who turn to us for help. We may not be able to meet every need, but when compassion compels us, we will amaze ourselves by doing more than we often allow.

A FRIEND IN DEED

Make time for a friend or acquaintance who reaches out today.

YET AGAIN

Do it again, Lord! Save us, O Lord, our God!
Gather us from our exile and unite us together
so that we will give our great
and joyous thanks to you again
and bring you glory by our praises.

PSALM 106:47 TPT

We cannot exhaust the mercy of God. He is full of lovingkindness and chance after chance in his abundant grace! May we never stop ourselves from turning to him. He will not reject us, and he won't ignore our pleas for help. When it comes down to it, what are we hoping for? Is it restoration, healing, or unity? Let's take a look at what lies beneath the cries of our heart.

As we cry out to the Lord, let's not neglect the cries of those around us asking for help. Let's partner with the heart of God in meeting needs with generosity. Let's be the reason that another rejoices, not only in the upcoming season of thanksgiving and charity but all year round!

A FRIEND IN DEED

When a friend asks for help, do what you can
no matter how many times you've helped before.

TELL YOUR STORY

Let the redeemed of the LORD
tell their story.

PSALM 107:2 NIV

Every person has a story to tell. In fact, everyone has multiple stories to share! What do you find yourself sharing with others when you are around them? What are the stories that you are known for, that your friends know by heart? We are often drawn to stories that are funny, tragic, or miraculous.

What stories remain untold? If you have a precious testimony of kindness, share it with someone today. If you have been the recipient of someone else's help in time of need, let it be a story you share in humility and gratitude, laying aside your pride of self-sufficiency. If you have a story of coming out of a dark time and surviving, let it be something you share. Spend some time thinking through what you want your loved ones to know and share it openly with them. Vulnerability is a beautiful and connective force.

A FRIEND IN DEED

*Share a testimony of goodness
that you have never shared before.*

NOVEMBER

"Love each other
as I have loved you.
Greater love has no one than this:
to lay down one's life
for one's friends."

John 15:12-13 NIV

PRAISE AND THANKS

Praise the LORD!
I will thank the LORD with all my heart
as I meet with his godly people.

PSALM 111:1 NLT

There is power in gratitude, not because it has some magical force, but because it directs our focus toward the blessings that are already ours. It is good not only to make a private practice of gratitude, but also to be intentional about it with others. As we enter into this season of thanksgiving, let's take note of the things we have to be grateful for.

The next time you are with a friend, a coworker, or a family member, make a point to share something that you are grateful for—including them! Think of the attributes that endear them to you and share it with them. Don't be afraid of how it will sound. Encouragement is a gift to everyone. Let this be the day you lean into the vulnerability of sharing what you love about people with them.

A FRIEND IN DEED

Make a point to share your gratitude with a friend today.

ACTS OF MERCY

His unforgettable works of surpassing wonder
reveal his grace and tender mercy.

PSALM 111:4 TPT

Have you ever been the recipient of someone else's grand gesture of kindness? Perhaps you received an unexpected gift, a bill was covered, or a thoughtful endorsement was spoken. Whatever it was, how did it make you feel? What were the emotions that coursed through you in response to their generosity?

God is gracious and merciful. He is abundant in love, and all that he does reflects his heart of redemption. May we take time to recognize what he has done and remember what others have sacrificed in love. These are tangible acts of goodness. Let's not forget the wonderful ways that mercy has kissed our lives and take hope in the fact that we haven't finished experiencing its miracles yet. Let's not neglect that as we partner with God's heart, we can graciously offer substantial kindness to others.

 A FRIEND IN DEED

Pay for someone's meal today.

ALWAYS TRUSTWORTHY

All he does is just and good,
and all his commandments are trustworthy.

PSALM 111:7 NLT

We are all just trying our best. Most people in our lives
are not looking for ways to hurt us. They are doing what
they know to do in order to live. God is perfect in love.
We already know that none of us are. We fail each other,
not because we want to but because we are finite beings
with limited understanding and scope. We operate out of
conditioning and survival mechanisms.

But God is greater! And there is so much grace to be found
in him. When we make space for others to mess up and
leave room to make up, we offer each other the gift of grace.
We don't have to be perfect in love to choose the loving way.
Let's look to the teachings of Jesus, the ways he encouraged
us to live, and to his example. Let's not give up growing in
compassion and choosing the path of his laid-down love.
He is always trustworthy, and we can rely on his wisdom
and help.

A FRIEND IN DEED

Give grace to a friend who hasn't met your expectations.

REMIND YOURSELF

Return to your rest, my soul,
for the LORD has been good to you.

PSALM 116:7 NIV

When we remember the things of our past, do we ruminate on what we did not get right? Do we struggle with shame over how we handled ourselves in situations we wish we could change? Do we regret the actions of others and how they wounded us? Most assuredly, most of us struggle with this at some point.

Let's be sure to remember the good as well as the hard. We have a human bias toward negativity, but that does not mean that we cannot take our thoughts captive. Let's open the doors in our hearts and minds that lead to memories of goodness, fulfillment, and love. Let's remember how good the Lord has been to us. Let's recall the kindness of our loved ones as well. There is as much, if not more, goodness within our memory banks as there is pain.

A FRIEND IN DEED

*Take time to remember a great time you
had with a friend and share it with them.*

REJOICE IN TODAY

This is the day which the LORD has made;
Let us rejoice and be glad in it.

PSALM 118:24 NASB

What difference would it make in our day if we chose to look for reasons to rejoice? Let's open ourselves to the possibility of goodness in the details of our day. As we work, let's pay attention to the gift of coworkers and spaces that allow us to succeed. Let's turn our attention to small delights: the laughter of a child, the smile of a stranger, the smell of fallen leaves outside, the way the sun filters through the trees.

Whenever you notice something that brings joy, take note of it. Let delight lead you. Whether it's with a whispered "thank you" or a thought that notes the significance of the simple, may you find that your heart expands in gratitude as you embrace what meets you today. Share your intention with someone and invite them to do the same. There are so many reasons to rejoice today. What are yours?

A FRIEND IN DEED

*Take note of the simple joys you find today
and share a few with a friend.*

REVIVED IN HOPE

Your promise revives me;
it comforts me in all my troubles.

PSALM 119:50 NLT

How have you felt hope revive in you? Was it through a reminder, a loving friend, or a forgotten promise fulfilled? Perhaps you can't put it into words, and that's ok. You don't have to know how or why something happens to acknowledge that there is great grace at work. You don't have to be able to explain what comforts you in order to be comforted.

Love does not lead us astray. It is a worthy pursuit, whether we are persevering through hard times or we are feeling the warm delight of satisfaction. Perhaps reviving in hope means embracing what is real now, while also believing in what is still possible. The presence of the Lord wraps us in comforting peace. As we rest in him, let's look for ways to spread peace to those in our lives.

A FRIEND IN DEED

Remind a friend of a dream they've had
as you witness them living with the fruit of it today.

WHAT WISDOM

Give thanks to the Creator
who made the heavens with wisdom!
His tender love for us continues on forever!

PSALM 136:5 TPT

Wisdom without love is like a ringing bell in the middle of the night. It is a nuisance to those who are trying to find their rest. Loving wisdom comes from a place of compassion. It is truth laced with kindness. We often put ideologies above relationships, and that is not the way of Christ. He always put people first, though he did not hold back from speaking words of truth. Loving truth starts in our hearts. We cannot control how people will respond; they crucified Christ after all. But he always led with love.

How do we speak to those people in our lives? Do we simply say it like it is, thinking honesty equates to loving truth? Sometimes it does to be sure. But if we don't have compassion in our hearts, then it doesn't matter what we say. May we lean into the presence of God, fill up on his love, and live from that place today.

A FRIEND IN DEED

*Don't hide from telling the truth
but do it with kindness in your heart.*

MADE BRAVE

On the day I called you, you answered me.
You made me strong and brave.

PSALM 138:3 NCV

An answered call for help brings tremendous relief. Imagine being stuck on the side of the road in the middle of nowhere, not knowing what to do or how to get out of the situation. If you called and received an answer that help was on the way, would it not give you courage to wait? Wouldn't it strengthen your confidence that you would be okay?

We live in a world with a lot of troubles. There are tragedies all around us; yet we are not helpless in all counts. When was the last time you reached out to fill a need for someone who was desperately waiting on help? When natural disasters strike, do we not applaud the crisis teams that go in to help in any way possible? Let's be people of action not just intention. Let's show up in practical ways to empower others in courage and strength.

A FRIEND IN DEED

*When you see someone in need of help,
offer whatever aid you can give.*

MENDING WOUNDS

He heals the wounds
of every shattered heart.

PSALM 147:3 TPT

There is probably not a single soul that has not experienced some sort of heartbreak. We encounter pain, loss, grief, and sorrow in this life. None can escape it. The promise of the gospel of Christ isn't that we become immune to pain. It's not that we somehow escape suffering in this life, but that there is one who heals, restores, redeems, and welcomes us into his kingdom of love. We have someone to go to in our pain, one who walks with us through it, and who mends our bleeding hearts.

Glory is coming. Wholeness is near. Jesus will wipe every tear from our eyes, and there will be no more suffering or pain in his eternal kingdom. For now, let's join with the heart of our God and look for ways to mend the brokenhearted and bind the wounds of our fellow sojourners.

A FRIEND IN DEED

*Pray for a friend who is going through heartbreak
and ask what you can do.*

ABSOLUTELY NOTHING

How great is our God!
There's absolutely nothing his power cannot accomplish,
and he has infinite understanding of everything.

PSALM 147:5 TPT

God has infinite understanding. What a reason to rest in him today! Though each new day dawns with possibility, it also progresses with unforeseen interruptions and setbacks. Let's not be discouraged by this, for what is a mystery to us is already known to God. He cannot be taken off guard. He already sees it all clearly. Let's trust him and look to his leadership.

Not only is God all-knowing, but he is also all powerful. There is nothing that his lifegiving strength cannot accomplish. We cannot imagine how our lives will unfold, but God is with us. He has more than enough power to demolish any and every wall that gets in the way of his purposes. Let's not give up hope; instead, let's lean on the wisdom of our mighty Creator and trust his faithfulness in all things.

A FRIEND IN DEED

Share an insight you've recently had with a friend.

IT IS TIME

Hallelujah! Praise the Lord!
It's time to sing to God a brand-new song
so that all his holy people will hear how wonderful he is!

PSALM 149:1 TPT

Today is the only day we have to seize. It is all that we are able to fully embrace. Let's not take any moment in our day for granted. Let's lean into the present, giving our energy to the things we can control, all the while trusting God with what we cannot control. It's time to take responsibility for what is ours to do. It's time to rise up in hope again. It's time.

Let's not let this day pass us by without looking for reasons to sing. There is as much purpose in pleasure as there is in pain. There is as much to gain from delight as there is from perseverance. Let's lean into the lightness of bright moments, singing our songs to the Lord and sharing ourselves with those around us. This is all we have; let's not waste it.

A FRIEND IN DEED

Connect with those who are important to you today.

INESCAPABLE GOODNESS

I can never escape from your Spirit!
I can never get away from your presence!
If I ride the wings of the morning,
if I dwell by the farthest oceans,
even there your hand will guide me,
and your strength will support me.

PSALM 139:7, 9-10 NLT

We cannot run from the presence of God. He is all around; he fills the universe. He does not leave us when we try to hide. He does not condemn us when we would condemn ourselves. His goodness is indescribable. His wonders are innumerable.

The Psalms are filled with poetic declarations to God. Some are raw and heart-wrenching. Others are celebratory and filled with the awe of the author's revelation. God can handle us just as we are, and he invites us to come to him without pretense. Let's offer him the reality of our hearts today. Let's invite him to move in his mercy and touch the places within our souls that are thirsty for his lifegiving waters.

A FRIEND IN DEED

Let a faraway friend know that you are thinking of them.

HE WILL NOT FAIL

> "I will be with you as I was with Moses.
> I will not fail you or abandon you.
> Be strong and courageous."

JOSHUA 1:5-6 NLT

Joshua needed an incredible dose of courage to walk out the role he had been given. As a leader, he became responsible for the nation of Israel. God promised to be with him, just as he had been with Moses. Whatever we are facing, whatever feels overwhelming, God is with us. He will not fail us nor abandon us. He will lead us even as we step into roles that feel intimidating.

Who are the supports and rocks that we lean on in life? What friends and mentors hold us up, remind us of who we are, and impart courage to our waning hearts when we need it? May we take time to acknowledge them, to thank them, and to be those friends and mentors to others. No matter what, God will not fail. Let's be friends who stick with each other through thick and thin and who encourage each other to trust the one who gave us to each other.

A FRIEND IN DEED

Encourage a friend who is stepping into a new role.

FREEDOM IS HERE

Let us praise the Lord, the God of Israel, because he has
come to help his people and has given them freedom.
He has given us a powerful Savior.

LUKE 1:68-69 NCV

Jesus came to bring help and freedom. In his redemption,
we find true liberty. His Spirit helps us when we don't know
what to do. His leadership guides us through the winding
path of this life, through the ups and downs. He is faithful
to save, restore, and redeem. He is faithful to heal, to revive,
and to comfort. He is faithful to his people and through him
we find freedom of fellowship with the Father of creation.

All who come to Christ are welcomed. All who call on him
are acknowledged. There isn't a person who cries out for
his help who is denied. Can we say the same? When others
reach out for help, are we able to show up or direct them to
where they can receive it? We are not helpless in this life.
All we have is a gift from a good Father, and sharing it is a
privilege. Let's liberate those in our lives with the gift of love
without condition. Even when it's hard, let's keep choosing
kindness instead of judgment.

A FRIEND IN DEED

Love your friends through the changes in their lives.

LIGHT IN DARKNESS

"Because of God's tender mercy,
the morning light from heaven
is about to break upon us,
to give light to those who sit in darkness
and in the shadow of death,
to guide us to the path of peace."

LUKE 1:78-79 NLT

God is able to do far more than we ever could. His love reaches further than we dare go. His kindness shows up in places we would never want to be found. Let's not limit the grace of God to our comfort zones. Let's allow God to be greater than our understanding and to let our perceptions be challenged by the power of his passion.

Do we look with compassion on those we know and love, yet harden our hearts against those we don't understand? Let's let the compassion of Christ crack open our hearts, so we see others through the lens of his love instead of through our own fears or criticisms. Will we allow the mercy of God to break our biases as we interact with those he loves completely and fully, as wholly as he loves us?

A FRIEND IN DEED

Ask God for help to connect with those you may seek to avoid.

INTRICATELY MADE

"You guided my conception
and formed me in the womb.
You clothed me with skin and flesh,
and you knit my bones and sinews together."

JOB 10:10-11 NLT

God is not just Creator of the world and all that is in it; he
is the artist who formed each of us in his image. We hold
a unique aspect of the Maker's mark in our beings. No one
is a mistake. No one is an afterthought. Each person was
lovingly and intricately made.

Do we view our imperfections with grace or with
contempt? Do we allow for the perceived weaknesses
we have to be what they are, or do we try to hide them
in whatever way possible? When we despise something
in ourselves, we cover it up with shame. But this doesn't
work in our favor, and it doesn't translate well in our
relationships either. Let's give each other the gift of our
humanity, of showing up as our whole selves complete with
the parts we like and the parts we are learning to accept.

A FRIEND IN DEED

Share an insecurity you have with a trusted friend.

ALL THAT IS WITHIN

Bless the LORD, O my soul,
and all that is within me,
bless his holy name!
Bless the LORD, O my soul,
and forget not all his benefits.

PSALM 103:1-2 ESV

May you take this opportunity to do this spiritual practice with the psalmist today. *Bless the Lord, Oh my soul, and all that is within me.* We can choose to bless the Lord, to offer him praise and thanks no matter what we are feeling in the moment. *Bless the Lord, Oh my soul, and forget not all his benefits.* We can choose to focus on what he has given, and how fellowship with him has enriched our lives.

The same principle also applies to our other relationships. No matter how we feel about the people in our lives at any given moment, we can turn our attention to focus on the ways that we are blessed for knowing them. Take time to think of a friend and remember what the benefits are for knowing them. List them out, whether in your mind or on paper, and consider how your perspective can be enriched.

A FRIEND IN DEED

When you are struggling with someone, take a moment to remember the things you like about them.

HE ALREADY KNOWS

The LORD is like a father to his children,
tender and compassionate to those who fear him.
For he knows how weak we are;
he remembers we are only dust.

PSALM 103:13-14 NLT

Hopefully, we do not look at our loved ones with eyes of perfection, thinking they can do no wrong. We already know that no one is perfect. This includes our friends, family, and strangers alike. Let's lean into the grace that God so readily gives us and offer mercy instead of judgment when others let us down and when we disappoint ourselves.

God is not taken aback by our failures. He knows that we are only dust. He does not hold our pasts against us when we ask forgiveness. He gives us fresh mercy, a clean slate, and an open embrace. Let's offer the loved ones in our lives grace, too, and allow for their imperfections as well as their strengths.

A FRIEND IN DEED

*Let a minor irritation or frustration with a friend go
without needing to bring attention to it.*

ALL ALONG

God you are near me always, so close to me;
every one of your commands reveals truth.
I've known all along how true and unchanging
is every word you speak, established forever!

PSALM 119:151-152 TPT

The Lord is steadfast and true; the best and most faithful friend we will ever find. When we feel utterly alone, let's remember that God does not abandon us no matter what we do. When our loved ones cannot understand what we are going through, he does. When no one else sees our pain, he is close in comfort.

As we travel the road of life, looking back we will find that he has been close all along. He never leaves us nor forsakes us. He will not turn away when we ask for help. He is present in the long, dark night. He is our peace in the storm. He is at work even in our greatest mess. He will never fail us, so let's hold tightly to his close grip and turn our attention to his nearness.

A FRIEND IN DEED

Ask Jesus to show you what friendship with him looks like.

WISDOM IN FRIENDSHIP

So stop fooling yourselves!
Evil companions will corrupt good morals and character.

1 CORINTHIANS 15:33 TPT

The character of the people we spend time with will affect our own choices over time. Let's be wise about who we choose as trusted companions and friends. Those who cheat, lie, and abuse others will not do anything to add goodness to our lives. Let's instead choose honest and trustworthy friends. People who are kind, compassionate, and reliable.

All relationships take time and attention, so let's make sure that we're giving it to people who will add value to our lives. A person does not have to know Christ to have good morals and character. A person who claims to be a Christian yet does not live like it is not better than someone who is not and aims to live with good values. In any case, we get to choose our friends and influences, so let's choose wisely!

A FRIEND IN DEED

Spend time with a kind friend today.

BETTER TOGETHER

Two people are better off than one,
for they can help each other succeed.

ECCLESIASTES 4:9 NLT

Have you been trying to reach a goal on your own? Have you been relying on self-motivation to get you through the hard days? We are not created to go it alone, and we thrive in the context of community. Even if you only have one friend you can touch base with about your goals and struggles, know that there is benefit in including others in your journey.

Perhaps you have already known the difference it makes to share your goals, your life, and your burdens with others. Think about how the support you have received has affected you. Has it helped you to go further than you could on your own? Has it lightened the load that threatened to overwhelm you? Whether this is already how you live or something you want to grow in, take the opportunity to reach out to the potential partners who are already in your life.

A FRIEND IN DEED

*Ask a friend to keep you accountable to your goals
and offer the same to them.*

REACH OUT

> If one person falls, the other can reach out and help.
> But someone who falls alone is in real trouble.
>
> ECCLESIASTES 4:10 NLT

It is important to know that we have others we can rely on in life. When the load gets too heavy and we don't know how we will go on, who are the people we turn to? Let's not give in to the lie that we must succeed or fail on our own. A friend is someone we can rely on even miles apart. May we never forget the power of encouragement, solidarity, and help when we most need it.

When we have times of smooth sailing, do we overlook the troubles that our friends are going through? Just as we need the help of others to lift us up, so our friends need that from us. If you find yourself in a steady season, take some time to think about your friends in different circumstances. Reach out to them today and check in on them. They may need a helping hand.

A FRIEND IN DEED

*Check in with a friend who is
in a time of uncertainty or hardship.*

DIFFERENT PARTS

If the whole body were an eye, it would not be able to hear.
If the whole body were an ear, it would not be able to smell.
If each part of the body were the same part, there would be
no body. But truly God put all the parts, each one of them,
in the body as he wanted them.

1 CORINTHIANS 12:17-18 NCV

Not only is there beauty in the diversity of people, cultures,
landscapes, and more, but there is also purpose in it. We
rely on water to hydrate us, food to nourish us, air to
sustain us, and sleep to restore us. We need the diverse
experiences of nature as well as the differing skills of the
people around us to thrive.

Paul says that the community of believers is like a body. We
cannot all seek to serve the same purpose, for we are meant
to use our unique gifts to support the rest of the body. How
often do you see someone's differences as their strength?
God did not make us carbon copies of each other or even of
himself. There is incredible opportunity for strength as we
learn to appreciate what we have to offer and to let others
rise up in what they have to offer as well.

A FRIEND IN DEED

*Tell a friend the strengths and differences
you appreciate about them.*

TRUSTED SECRETS

A useless person causes trouble,
and a gossip ruins friendships.

PROVERBS 16:28 NCV

Are we trustworthy sources for our friends' secrets? When
something is shared in confidence and the confider is
not in any danger, then we should keep it to ourselves.
When we talk to our friends about others, let's not drag
anyone's name through the mud. Let's lead with compassion
and grace even when others are not present. May we be
trustworthy at all times no matter who is or isn't around us.

Gossip can ruin a friendship. When there is a rampant
need to know others' business without having the trusted
relationship to carry it, the propensity to make assumptions
about what others' actions mean, jumping to conclusions
without the information of intention, and carelessness
about other people in general, there will be mistrust. May
we rise above this and be arbiters of honesty, trust, grace,
and love.

A FRIEND IN DEED

*Thank a trusted friend for the ability to open up
in vulnerability with them.*

COMING AND GOING

The LORD keeps you from all harm
and watches over your life.
The LORD keeps watch over you as you come and go,
both now and forever.

PSALM 121:7-8 NLT

Friends will come and go. Some will stick with us for the long haul, but others will move away, or we will drift apart as our lives change. Though there is grief that accompanies this change, it is not a failure. The Lord watches over us as we come and go, and he will not leave us alone in any of it.

Is there a friend that you've been trying to remain as close to as you once were? Perhaps it is time to loosen the reins a bit. It is okay to make room for connections that are present, all the while honoring the relationship that you had, or continue to have, with old friends. Relationships change. We may grow apart in some ways and remain connected in others. Let's make sure that we are first and foremost rooted in love, and let's evaluate where to give our relational energy in this season of our lives.

A FRIEND IN DEED

Lean into the friendships that feel easy on your soul.

REFRESHING RELATIONSHIPS

Sweet friendships refresh the soul
and awaken our hearts with joy,
for good friends are like the anointing oil
that yields the fragrant incense of God's presence.

PROVERBS 27:9 TPT

The most refreshing relationships in our lives are the ones that feel effortless not because they actually are, but because we have put time into getting to know each other, support each other, and uplift each other. Sweet friendships reflect the beauty found in God's presence. How wonderful is that?

When you think about your sweetest friendships, what comes to mind? Who are your people? What is it like to be around them? Take some time to write down the attributes of refreshing relationships and thank God for how they reflect his goodness. There is even more kindness, revival, and life in his presence. Let's give more time to those who inspire and revive us and let's build them into the rhythm of our lives.

A FRIEND IN DEED

Give a sweet friend a call
and plan to spend time together soon.

LOYAL COMPANIONS

Elijah said to Elisha, "Stay here;
the LORD has sent me to Bethel."
But Elisha said, "As surely as the LORD lives and as you live,
I will not leave you." So they went down to Bethel.

2 KINGS 2:2 NIV

Even in the times when we think we can go it alone, it is always good to have the support of a loyal friend. Ruth did the same thing with Naomi. Naomi was going back to her homeland, and she told her daughter-in-law to return to her own country. But Ruth couldn't bear the thought of being separated from Naomi. She did not leave her, and in the end, they were both blessed because of her loyal companionship.

Are there friends with whom you would go to the ends of the earth? Who are the friends that would not leave you even when it seemed like a good idea that they should? These are loyal companions, faithful friends, and beautiful pictures of God's faithfulness. Praise God if you have someone like this in your life. Ask for the gift of friendship if you don't have it yet!

A FRIEND IN DEED

Buy a thoughtful gift for a loyal friend.

FAMILIAR

You discern my going out and my lying down;
  you are familiar with all my ways.
Before a word is on my tongue,
  you, LORD, know it completely.

PSALM 139:3-4 NIV

What a relief it is to be known by others. When our friends are familiar with our ways, there is a comfort to not having to explain ourselves. This doesn't happen overnight. It happens through a lot of conversations, time together, and context. These friends seem to know what we are thinking before we say anything. What a gift it is to be known in such a way.

Who are you most familiar with? When you think about your close relationships, how do you feel? May we have reciprocal relationships with friends where we are each known, loved, and cared for. Every one of us deserves that kind of acceptance.

A FRIEND IN DEED

Buy a gift based on an inside joke for a close friend.

EVERYONE'S TALKING

Your awe-inspiring acts of power
have everyone talking!
And I'm telling people everywhere
about your excellent greatness!

PSALM 145:6 TPT

If you could brag on a friend in any way, telling others about the amazing traits they uphold, what would you say? Consider talking them up today, sharing the things that come to mind. Don't just share it with others, but also make sure that you tell your friend what you know and love about them as well.

In the same way, what do you want your friends to say about you? If they were to describe what makes you a good friend, what would they say? If there seems to be a disconnect between what you want to be true and what seems to be true, take some time to put intention into action. You can change how you show up in relationships. Even small movements and shifts matter.

A FRIEND IN DEED

Brag on a friend's amazing qualities today.

FIRMLY ESTABLISHED

Tremble before Him, all the earth.
The world also is firmly established,
It shall not be moved.
Let the heavens rejoice,
and let the earth be glad;
and let them say among the nations,
"The LORD reigns."

1 CHRONICLES 16:30-31 NKJV

Have you ever met someone whose company felt like home? Perhaps you have known them for a long time, or you met and just seemed to click. There are many different types of friends in this life, but the ones who feel like home, no matter where we are, are the ones who give us a glimpse into the firmly established kingdom of Christ.

Friends like this are reason to rejoice! May we not take them for granted or lose sight of the importance of spending time with them. Let's nurture these friendships, giving time to be refreshed and encouraged. A strong connection needs to be nourished, so let's take time to feed the important relationships in our lives.

A FRIEND IN DEED

*Reach out to a friend who feels like home
and tell them that you love them.*

DECEMBER

Do not be fooled:
"Bad friends
will ruin good habits."

1 CORINTHIANS 15:33 NCV

EYES FIXED

I keep my eyes always on the LORD.
With him at my right hand, I will not be shaken.
Therefore my heart is glad and my tongue rejoices;
my body also will rest secure.

PSALM 16:8-9 NIV

As we enter this season of Advent, remembering the birth of our Lord Jesus Christ, let's turn our attention to the mystery and wonder of his presence with us. Let's fix our eyes on him, the author and perfecter of our faith. He is the Son of God, who clothed himself in flesh and humbled himself to become vulnerable in humanity. He did it all because he was compelled to reveal the merciful heart of the Father to a world in desperate need.

When we know how wholly we are loved, does it not give us confidence in every area of life? We can rest assured that God will not leave us. Jesus has made a way for us to know the liberty of the Father's love and has given us his Spirit who is always near. As we keep our eyes on the Lord, may we find that our relationships are enriched in a love that knows no end.

A FRIEND IN DEED

Spend time with a friend who gives you confidence.

BLESSED TO TRUST

Blessed is the man who trusts in the LORD,
And whose hope is the LORD.

JEREMIAH 17:7 NKJV

Even when our friends let us down, God never will. He is
faithful in the details as well as in the grand scheme. We
cannot expect perfection from our friends and loved ones,
but we can rely on the perfect faithfulness of the Lord.
Instead of letting our frustrations with broken expectations
lead us to pull back from our loved ones, let's extend grace
and be honest about it. We have to communicate our
own process to some degree if we want someone else to
understand us. God can read our hearts, but unfortunately,
no one else can.

Trust can be built in reparation and restoration after
disappointment. But if we don't give others the opportunity
to know how they affected us, there is no way to get there.
Some things we can simply let go of, but for the things that
truly wound us, we should communicate those. Let's give
mercy a chance to build bridges and give those we trust the
opportunity to rise up.

A FRIEND IN DEED

Share how someone's actions affected you.

PATH OF PROMISE

God's way is perfect.
All the LORD's promises prove true.
He is a shield for all who look to him for protection.
For who is God except the LORD?
Who but our God is a solid rock?

PSALM 18:30-31 NLT

When we are in the waiting seasons of life, the thing that can make the biggest difference in the quality of that time is those who wait with us. There are some dreams for which we labor an inordinate amount of time before they are reached. There are some hopes that cannot be worked into existence. Those who sit with us and walk with us on the journey can encourage and lighten the load.

When was the last time you listened to someone else's story of a dream fulfilled? There are testimonies of God's goodness everywhere—not as blueprints but as reminders that God moves in miracles of mercy that are as unique as each of us. He will not quit, and he won't fail. Let's lean into hope and trust the one who weaves it all together.

A FRIEND IN DEED

Share a testimony of goodness with a friend
who is struggling with discouragement.

GOOD NEWS OF GREAT JOY

The angel said to them, "Do not be afraid. I bring you good news that will cause great joy for all the people. Today in the town of David a Savior has been born to you; he is the Messiah, the Lord."

LUKE 2:10-11 NIV

What is the best news you've heard lately? Is there a report of good news that has given you great joy? Even if you find yourself still waiting for relief and full of fear, trust that a breakthrough is coming. Let the Spirit of peace flood you with his presence. He is near, and he drives out fear with perfect love.

Let's remember the news that the angels spread, not only to Mary but to shepherds and astrologers as well. He doesn't leave anyone out of his plan. Everyone is welcome, all who hear the good news of Christ can find joy in him. He is not the Savior of the few but of all. Let's look to him as our hope, our fulfillment, and our harbinger of goodness.

A FRIEND IN DEED

When you hear good news, share it with friends!

PEOPLE OF GOD

"Sing and rejoice, O daughter of Zion! For behold, I am coming and I will dwell in your midst," says the LORD. "Many nations shall be joined to the LORD in that day, and they shall become My people. And I will dwell in your midst. Then you will know that the LORD of hosts has sent Me to you."

ZECHARIAH 2:10-11 NKJV

Though we live in a world where sorrow and suffering are inescapable, there are also glorious glimpses of hope all around. The Lord of hosts came to earth; he struggled, he overcame, and he ministered to the masses. He healed, he encouraged, and he set captives free. He lived, he died, and he rose again. He still heals, encourages, comforts, and liberates. He saves and redeems as powerfully as he ever has.

The presence of the Spirit of God is in our midst. He has made his home within us. We are not waiting for him to come. He has already entered the home of our hearts as we submit our lives his leadership. He dwells with us: our closest friend and confidant, our loyal companion and liberator. He is here now, breaking chains and reviving our hearts in hope.

Connect with a community of believers.

TIME OF SINGING

"The flowers appear on the earth,
the time of singing has come."

SONG OF SOLOMON 2:12 ESV

Have you ever been startled by love? Whether it's the love of a friend, partner, parent, or child, how did it revive you in ways you didn't even know you needed? When we come out of seasons of sorrow, barrenness, or disappointment, after grief has moved through us, the invitation of a loved one can be the most refreshing wave of hope.

Just as winter gives way to spring, so will sadness give way to singing. The buds of flowers, painting the landscape with splashes of renewal, will give way to lush gardens of life. If you find yourself in a spiritual or emotional winter, know that spring will come. Relief will come. Treasure the moments of life and love you have now and hold on until tomorrow comes.

A FRIEND IN DEED

Share a seed of hope with a friend.

SELF-CONTROL

The grace of God has appeared that offers salvation to all
people. It teaches us to say "No" to ungodliness and worldly
passions, and to live self-controlled, upright and Godly lives
in this present age.

TITUS 2:11-12 NIV

When you think of self-control, what comes to mind? Is it
personal practices that add to your health or does it also
apply to your relationships? Perhaps the greatest test of
our self-control has to do with how we relate to others.
When we would rather throw out a harsh retort, choosing
self-control means holding back careless words based in
defensiveness.

Self-control starts within us. It begins with intention and
is followed through with action. Let's not overlook the
responsibility we have over our choices. Let's remember
how our carelessness can affect those we love. As we
practice self-control, it comes more naturally. Let's go
into our interactions today with grace, kindness, and
mindfulness.

A FRIEND IN DEED

Choose your words wisely when in a disagreement.

ROCK OF STRENGTH

No one is holy like the LORD!
There is no one besides you;
there is no Rock like our God.

1 SAMUEL 2:2 NLT

Is there someone in your life you refer to as a rock? Someone who is steady and faithful, always reliable, and there when you need them? They may seem unflappable in chaos. No matter what is going on in your life, they are ready to go through it with you. There is strength in this kind of solidarity, knowing that you don't go it alone in any storm.

This type of friend is a gift, but let's remember that we are only human! Everyone will face their own storms in life, and when they do, may we show up ready to lend our support. Even when people fail, let us look to the rock who never moves and who is always ready to rescue us—our God! When we cannot be near those we wish could be present, let us pray for the strength of the Lord to fill them.

A FRIEND IN DEED

*Send a handwritten note of encouragement
and thanks to a faithful friend.*

PRAY FOR NEEDS

First, I tell you to pray for all people. Ask God for the things
people need, and be thankful to him. You should pray for
kings and for all who have authority. Pray for the leaders
so that we can have quiet and peaceful lives—lives full of
worship and respect for God.

1 TIMOTHY 2:1-2 NLT

How often do we pray for other people's needs and not
just our own? Prayer is a powerful practice to adjust our
focus and surrender our helplessness to the King of kings
and Lord of lords. Let's not neglect praying for those in
leadership, for those we struggle to get along with, and for
those who are suffering without knowing when reprieve
will come.

Let's not forget the power of prayer, not only for ourselves
but for others. When we focus our hearts and minds
on Jesus Christ, on his resurrection power, and on his
inescapable mercy, the problems of this life are put into
perspective. Let's press into him today and pray for others
as we do.

A FRIEND IN DEED

*Pray for the power of God to break through
in your friends' lives.*

DWELLING PLACE OF REST

God's dwelling place is now among the people, and he will dwell with them. "He will wipe every tear from their eyes. There will be no more death" or mourning or crying or pain, for the old order of things has passed away.

REVELATION 21:4 NIV

Perfect rest will come to us one day as we enter into the fullness of God's kingdom. Until then, we have glimpses of this glorious peace in fellowship with Christ through his Spirit. What a wonderful day it is to look forward to: the removal of death, of grief, of pain. As we wait for that magnificent reality, may we not overlook the moments we experience the beauty of his comfort, his kindness, and his grace.

What would it do for our families, our communities, and our culture if God's people became dwelling places of rest for the hurting and broken? What if we were as hospitable to the poor and the sick as Jesus himself was? When love drives us, we will find that the cost of our own comfort is not enough to satisfy. Let's make our homes places of rest, but let's also offer that rest to others.

A FRIEND IN DEED

Offer someone a break from their pain by giving them something that focuses on their rest.

BEST FRIENDS

The Lord is my best friend and my shepherd.
I always have more than enough.
He offers a resting place for me in his luxurious love.
His tracks take me to an oasis of peace,
the quiet brook of bliss.

PSALM 23:1-2 TPT

Take some time today to focus on the one who never leaves you. Lean into the friendship that always offers support, peace, joy, and rest. Friendship with the Lord is full of fruitfulness. It is not an afterthought but the primary source of our strength.

Read through Psalm 23 and invite the Lord to move in your heart. Ask for his wisdom where you have confusion. Invite him to guide you in spaces that feel cloudy and dark. There is nothing he cannot do for you, but most of all, he wants you to know him, to experience his love, and to trust him. When you do that, your heart will lead you to follow him wherever he leads. Nurture your friendship today, and you will find that he is already working within you.

A FRIEND IN DEED

Spend time in the presence of the Lord.

SO VERY NEAR

"I am a God who is near," says the LORD.
"I am also a God who is far away.
No one can hide where I cannot see him," says the LORD.
"I fill all of heaven and earth," says the LORD.

JEREMIAH 23:23-24 NCV

In our closest friendships, we cannot hide a hard time. We cannot cover over a season of depression. Our friends know us well, and they can sense changes within us whether we voice them or not. Instead of trying to get by in silence, let's share what we feel we are able to share. Let's invite our trusted friends into the process even if we don't have words to articulate exactly what we are going through.

Support doesn't have to understand fully. It is the strength of showing up, of being there. Let's be near our friends. Let's show up even if we feel helpless. Let's be the ones who pick up the kids, drop off the meals, and sit with each other on couches or in waiting rooms. Let's be the hands and feet of Christ.

A FRIEND IN DEED

Order dinner for a friend who is overwhelmed.

COME CLOSE

I come to your altar, O LORD,
singing a song of thanksgiving
and telling of all your wonders.

PSALM 26:6-7 NLT

When was the last time we truly took the time to thank our closest people for their friendship? The ones who have seen us through the long nights and even longer mornings. The ones who celebrate our smallest wins and show up to cheer us on as we run races. Just as we sing songs of thanksgiving to the Lord who does wonderful things, let's not neglect the importance of singing the praise of our faithful friends.

God is not offended when we celebrate the people in our lives. He takes joy in our jubilation! He is a delight-filled God who loves when we love. It is so important for us to acknowledge the hard things in life, but it is even more important to recognize where the light filters in, where joys spring up, and where mercy is shown. Let's celebrate our loved ones and let's not hold back our thanks today.

A FRIEND IN DEED

*Take a beloved friend out to celebrate your friendship
and tell them how thankful you are for them.*

SEEK AND FIND

> "You will call on me and come and pray to me,
> and I will listen to you.
> You will seek me and find me
> when you seek me with all your heart."
>
> JEREMIAH 29:12–13 NIV

Where has your heart been directing you lately? Where have you found your attention going? What are the things you have been seeking after? When we take time to consider these things, we may find that we are not putting our energy into the things or people we actually value the most. Relationships take intention and follow through. They require time and attention.

If we find ourselves off balance in our relationships, wanting to develop some but not actually putting our attention to it, then let's take this opportunity to reevaluate our priorities. Once we have done this, we can make a game plan of small daily steps to get us closer to our goals, both in relationships and in life. When we seek something with all our hearts, we will find it. What are our hearts searching for?

A FRIEND IN DEED

Send an update to a friend who lives far away.

SOJOURNERS

"Who am I and who are my people that we should be able to offer as generously as this? For all things come from You, and from Your hand we have given You. For we are sojourners before You, and tenants, as all our fathers were; our days on the earth are like a shadow, and there is no hope."

1 CHRONICLES 29:14-15 NASB

When we recognize that this life is a time of passing through as our mothers and fathers did before us and theirs before them, we can get a grip on our main aims in the short time we have. Time passes whether we mark it or not. People come and they go, leaving their mortal bodies behind. Their memories remain alive in us.

Let's not waste today by overly focusing on things that don't matter. Let's build stronger relationships. Let's laugh with our loved ones. Let's take walks with our friends and neighbors. Let's eat together, play games, and love each other well. Any time spent with our beloved family and friends is not a moment wasted. Let's enjoy each other while we still can.

A FRIEND IN DEED

Finish your work earlier than usual and meet up with a friend.

CLEARED OF JUDGMENT

The LORD has taken away the judgments against you; he has cleared away your enemies. The King of Israel, the LORD, is in your midst; you shall never again fear evil. On that day it shall be said to Jerusalem: "Fear not, O Zion; let not your hands grow weak."

ZEPHANIAH 3:15-18 ESV

What an amazing gift it is that Christ has taken away our judgments! Everything that could have been held against us is covered in his mercy. Though we may have to walk out the consequences of our actions in our relationships and in life, he does not hold any of our sins against us. What a weight lifted! What a relief! Even if no one else on this earth forgives us, God does.

When we submit to the Lord, his lavishly luxurious love covers us completely. We are made new in him. May we be as gracious as the Lord has been to us. May we offer new chances of restoration and mercy to those seeking forgiveness. Let's leave behind the judgments of the past and look at what is true here and now.

A FRIEND IN DEED

Seek restoration with a friend you have been estranged from.

EVEN THOUGH

Even though the fig trees have no blossoms,
and there are no grapes on the vines;
even though the olive crop fails,
and the fields lie empty and barren;
even though the flocks die in the fields,
and the cattle barns are empty,
yet I will rejoice in the LORD!
I will be joyful in the God of my salvation!

HABAKKUK 3:17-18 NLT

When nothing seems to be going right, do we still rejoice in the Lord? This is when praise can be a sacrifice: offering what we do not readily have to give in the moment because the one who receives it deserves it.

God is as good in the drought as he is in the harvest. He is as faithful in winter as he is in summer. He is loyal in love, always providing for our needs. Let's offer him our praise both in and out of season. Let's never stop telling of his wonderful nature!

A FRIEND IN DEED

Remind a friend of how you've seen God work through them.

THINK OF THIS

I have hope when I think of this:
The LORD's love never ends;
his mercies never stop.
They are new every morning.

Lamentations 3:21-23 NCV

No matter what yesterday looked like, no matter how the day might have been, today dawned with new mercy. There is a fresh portion of grace to drink from. There is more than enough love here in this moment. You are surrounded by it. You are filled with the light of God's Spirit who makes his home in you.

When things feel overwhelming, turn your attention to the peace of God within. Reach out with an open heart and invite the Lord to move in you. Ask for a fresh dose of his patience, his kindness, his wisdom, and his perspective. When you don't know how you will get through a meeting, an unforeseen appointment, or simply through the day, know that you are not alone. Ask the Lord for his strength in your weakness and ask a friend for prayer.

A FRIEND IN DEED

Offer to pray for a friend over the phone or in person.

QUIET CONFIDENCE

The LORD is good to those who depend on him,
to those who search for him.
So it is good to wait quietly
for salvation from the LORD.

LAMENTATIONS 3:25-26 NLT

When we know the nature of the people we depend upon, we can gather our confidence, or lack thereof, based on that information. God is faithful. He is merciful. He is good. We don't have to worry about whether God will come through on his promises. He will. We can rely on him because he is trustworthy.

What about your character? Can your friends and loved ones count on you? Do you follow through on your word? Are you available to help when something goes wrong? Are you ready to celebrate when a friend has reason to rejoice? Think about one way you want to be known. Ask the Lord to help you encourage that trait and ask him for wisdom to implement a pattern in your life to promote it.

A FRIEND IN DEED

Return a favor to a friend who came through for you recently.

GETTING BY

I lie down and sleep;
I wake again,
because the Lord sustains me.

PSALM 3:3-4 NIV

The fact that you are reading this right now is the grace of
God. The one who knit you in your mother's womb is the
one who sustains you. Have you felt alone in a struggle?
Have you been just trying to get by? It's okay to not be able
to do all the things you see others doing. It's okay to go at
your own pace, thanking the Lord for life and breath. It's
okay to not be at your best.

Do you have a friend who doesn't feel good enough because
they are struggling in an area of their lives? How can you
encourage them to be gracious with themselves just as they
would with their loved ones? Perhaps you can be a voice of
encouragement to them today, knowing that when you are
in your own hard time, they can return the favor.

A FRIEND IN DEED

*Tell a friend how much you appreciate who they are
apart from anything they do.*

LIFE OF PRAYER

Let joy be your continual feast. Make your life a prayer.
And in the midst of everything be always giving thanks,
for this is God's perfect plan for you in Christ Jesus.

1 THESSALONIANS 5:16-18 TPT

When we don't know how to pray, let our lives speak for
themselves. We don't need words for our hearts to open up
and commune with the living God. He reads our hearts; he
knows what we cannot articulate. Perhaps we could simply
live and let that be enough.

Think of a faithful friend, someone you admire greatly.
What is it about them that you look up to? Is it the words
they speak, or is it how you see them living that impacts
you the most? A life with openhearted surrender to love
is never wasted. When we align our hearts and minds in
Christ, our actions will show it.

A FRIEND IN DEED

Tell a respected friend what you admire about how they live.

FRUIT THAT LASTS

The fruit of the Spirit is love, joy, peace, patience, kindness, goodness, faithfulness, gentleness, self-control; against such things there is no law.

GALATIANS 5:22-23 ESV

Hopefully, our relationships show the fruit of God's Spirit as much as any other area of our lives. Love, patience, kindness, faithfulness, and gentleness are best displayed in our interactions with others. Do our friends know us to be people of peace, following through on our word and practicing self-control?

The Word of God says that there is no law against the fruit of the Spirit. When we act in kindness, spreading love and joy, who can say a bad thing against us? But even if they do, the Lord will honor our choices. Let's choose the fruit that lasts, the fruit that gives life, encouragement, and hope to others. Let's choose to walk in the Spirit and live by his love. Everything that is sown in his mercy will reap a harvest when it is time.

A FRIEND IN DEED

*Encourage a friend who shows
the fruit of the Spirit in their lives.*

SHAMELESS JOY

David danced with all his might before the LORD. He had
on a holy linen vest. David and all the Israelites shouted
with joy and blew the trumpets as they brought the Ark of
the LORD to the city.

2 SAMUEL 6:14-15 NCV

David did not just dance with all his might before the Lord;
he did it in what we would consider his underwear. He was
completely unashamed; perhaps making a fool of himself
because of how overjoyed he was before the Lord. Have you
ever been so excited that you couldn't keep it to yourself,
and you didn't care what it looked like? This is the kind of
joy David was experiencing.

Rejoicing is best done in the company of others. When
others can join in our celebration, it makes it that much
more meaningful. Let's not overlook the importance of
celebrating both small and big wins in life with others. Even
the gift of life is reason enough to rejoice, for who knows
what tomorrow will bring?

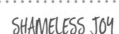

A FRIEND IN DEED

Celebrate life with a group of good friends.

RESTFUL RETREAT

The apostles returned to Jesus from their ministry tour and told him all they had done and taught. Then Jesus said, "Let's go off by ourselves to a quiet place and rest awhile." He said this because there were so many people coming and going that Jesus and his apostles didn't even have time to eat.

MARK 6:30–31 NLT

Jesus knew the importance of retreat and rest. When his apostles returned from their ministry trip, Jesus invited them to go away with him: away from the crowds and the demands. In a secluded and quiet place, they could rest and restore.

When was the last time you retreated from the demands of your life? Did you go with anyone close to you? Perhaps you can get away from the craziness of your life and plan a time with a close friend. If you can't get away for more than a day, plan some undistracted time with them for a few hours. Get out of your normal lives and away from the pressures. Follow the lead of Jesus and rest in the company of good friends, so you may be revived when you return.

A FRIEND IN DEED

Plan one-on-one time with a close friend.

CHAMPION FRIEND

To the fatherless he is a father.
To the widow he is a champion friend.
To the lonely he makes them part of a family.
To the prisoners he leads into prosperity
until they sing for joy.

PSALM 68:5-6 TPT

God is truly the best friend we could ever dream of having. He fills every role that is left unfulfilled in our lives and steps in as the perfect portion. He is a good and faithful Father to the fatherless. He is a champion friend and advocate to the widow. He welcomes the lonely into his family. He leads the prisoners out of their captivity into his generous joy!

The goodness of God cannot be overstated. Do we hold back our praise? The goodness of true friends also cannot be exaggerated. Let's be sure to tell our loved ones how much we appreciate them today. Let's learn to celebrate others' strengths! Let's uplift each other without it feeling weird. Encouragement is lifeblood to the struggling heart. Let's not hold back our genuine affection from anyone in our lives.

A FRIEND IN DEED

Thank a friend who has advocated for you with others.

TRUE FASTING

"Is not this the kind of fasting I have chosen:
Is it not to share your food with the hungry
and to provide the poor wanderer with shelter—
when you see the naked, to clothe them,
and not to turn away from your own flesh and blood?"

ISAIAH 58:6–7 NIV

Our spiritual practices do not amount to much of anything if they do not impact the way we live. If others are not affected by them, then what is the true use? No religious discipline will replace the need to show mercy, stand for justice, and help those in need. Let's consider how our spirituality reflects in these ways.

God is not impressed by our offerings, and he is not offended by our leaning into love. Let's make sure that we are not simply using our beliefs to maintain a comfortable life. Let's be sure that mercy is moving us to help house those who are homeless, feed those who are hungry, and fill a need when we are able. We cannot do everything, but we can certainly do something!

A FRIEND IN DEED

Offer to fill a need for a friend.

WORDS TO LIVE BY

Render true judgments, show kindness and mercy to one
another, do not oppress the widow, the fatherless, the
sojourner, or the poor, and let none of you devise evil
against another in your heart.

ZECHARIAH 7:8-10 ESV

This verse and these words stand on their own. They are
the gospel summed up. In Micah 6:8, a similar sentiment
is shared: "He has told you, O man, what is good; and what
does the Lord require of you but to do justice, and to love
kindness, and to walk humbly with your God?"

They also reflect the words of Jesus when he said,
"Whatever you wish that others would do to you, do also to
them" (Matthew 7:12). There is room for all in the kingdom
of Christ: room for those who have less to be taken care of
by those who have resources to spare, and room for love to
cover over a multitude of sins. Let's join with the heart of
God and make this a motto to live by!

A FRIEND IN DEED

*Stand on the side of the weak and vulnerable
when the opportunity arises.*

LOOK AROUND

When I consider Your heavens, the work of Your fingers,
the moon and the stars, which you have ordained,
what is man that You are mindful of him,
and the son of man that You visit him?

PSALM 8:3-4 NKJV

Take a walk outside and notice your surroundings. Take note of how the air enters your lungs. What does it feel like? What sounds draw your attention from your wandering thoughts? Is there birdsong, wind rustling through the trees, or the sound of crunching snow underfoot? When we take time to reach outside of ourselves and really notice the world around us, our perspective can shift. We are but a small part of a larger whole.

Though the world around us is big, we are connected to it through the places we go, the things we do, and our interactions with others. May we never forget how important it is to connect to others. Let's meet our people outside: hiking, walking, or having a snowball fight. When we spend time in nature with those we love, we can experience the wonder together.

A FRIEND IN DEED

Go on a walk with a friend.

TO KNOW IS TO TRUST

The LORD defends those who suffer;
he defends them in times of trouble.
Those who know the LORD trust him,
because he will not leave those who come to him.

PSALM 9:9-10 NCV

Those who know the Lord know that he is trustworthy. He proves faithful to all who depend on him. He is a defender of the weak and a support to those who suffer. He is loyal to those who have nowhere to turn. He never turns away a seeking heart. May we be loyal friends to those who depend on us. May we be people who reflect the steadfastness of the Lord in the ways we show up for those in our lives.

Who do you trust the most in your life? Let's not take for granted the faithful friends who show up for us time and time again. There is a blessing in sharing a load with others. Even when no one can fix our problems, knowing we're not alone in it is a great help.

A FRIEND IN DEED

Stand up for your friends when the opportunity arises.

UNFAILING LOVE

It is good to give thanks to the LORD,
to sing praises to the Most High.
It is good to proclaim your unfailing love in the morning,
your faithfulness in the evening.

PSALM 92:1-2 NLT

As you consider how your relationships have grown and changed this last year, write down the things you don't want to forget. How did compassion move you closer to your friends? How did choosing to listen to those who are different impact your worldview? What are the things you are grateful for? Who are the people you cherish?

Let your gratitude lead you to giving thanks to the Lord today. He is full of mercy, unfailing love, and faithfulness. He will not fail you, and the work he has already started in your heart and in your relationships will continue. Look to him today, offering him the gratitude and the openness of your heart. Let him show you the ways you did not even know he was working as you discover his kind perspective.

A FRIEND IN DEED

Tell a friend how grateful you are for them.

ALL IN HIS HANDS

The LORD is a great God, and a great King above all gods.
In his hand are the depths of the earth;
the heights of the mountains are his also.
The sea is his, for he made it,
and his hands formed the dry land.

PSALM 95:3-5 ESV

No matter how this year has turned out, there is more ahead. The start of a new year can bring fresh revelation of the mercy of God that makes everything new! What are you looking to leave behind you as the calendar turns over? Every day is a new opportunity to lay down what doesn't serve you and to trust your good Father to guide you into his goodness.

Though there are many mysteries *in* God, there are no mysteries *to* him. He sees everything clearly, and he is not worried. Will you trust him with your plans and with your relationships? Will you continue to follow his leadership as you clothe yourself with his compassion? Wherever you go, he is there already. He has a table prepared for you no matter the changes that come your way.

A FRIEND IN DEED

Wish your friends a Happy New Year!